THE EXTERNAL COMBUSTION ENGINE

FUTUREPOEM BOOKS
NEW YORK CITY
2005

THE EXTERNAL COMBUSTION ENGINE

MICHAEL IVES

FIRST EDITION | FIRST PRINTING

This edition first published in paperback by Futurepoem books
Futurepoem books, P.O. Box 34, New York, NY 10014
www.futurepoem.com
Editor: Dan Machlin
2003/2004 Guest Editors: Edwin Torres, Heather Ramsdell, Kristin Prevallet

Design: Anthony Monahan (am@anthonymonahan.com)
Cover Images © Anthony Monahan

Text set in Scala.
Printed in the United States of America on acid-free paper.

NYSCA

This book was made possible, in part, by grants from the New York State
Council on the Arts Literature Program, Fractured Atlas, the New York
Community Trust, and the Fund for Poetry. Futurepoem receives non-
profit sponsorship for grants and donations through Fractured Atlas
Productions, Inc., a non-profit 501(c)3 organization. Contributions are
fully tax-deductible and much needed!

Distributed to the trade by Small Press Distribution, Berkeley, California
Toll-free number (U.S. only): 800.869.7553
Bay area/International: 510.524.1668
orders@spdbooks.org
www.spdbooks.org

Some of the work in this book has appeared in the following publications:

3rd Bed: "The Four Fingers of the Left Hand," "Kenosis," "The Skeptic's Anatomical Parable . . ."

American Letters and Commentary: "Description of a Monument," "Origin of the Classical Orders," "Cooking the Distance"

Bridge: "The Fecundation," "Fughetta," "Turf Farming," the "Helot Parable" (from "The Seizure")

Can We Have Our Ball Back?: "Void Playing Off Solid Playing Off Void"

Conjunctions: "And to Explain the Achievement of Consciousness," "Gong Drops"

Denver Quarterly: "Bomb Dream"

elimae: "The Internal Combustion Engine," "Exuviae of the Chitinous," "Cognomen," "Curriculum Reform," "Reverse Phoenix"

Exquisite Corpse: "Précis of Historical Consciousness," "A Flower Blooms in Waco," "*Not Quite* Follows"

Fence: "The Dorian Invasions"

Matter: "The Annunciation"

Mississippi Review Online: "A Secularization"

Octopus: "Softening the Stone"

The Styles: "First Communion," "Brief Lecture on the Spectrum of Awareness," "The Question Concerning Technology," "Allegorical Portrait . . ."

Unsaid: "Pleroma," "The Ego and its Defenses," "It was a holiday and the sun shone unblemished—"

Brief passages from "Gong Drops" also appeared (in slightly different form) in *Exquisite Corpse*, *Slope*, and *Hunger*.

Thanks to Edwin Torres, Kristin Prevallet, Heather Ramsdell, and Dan Machlin.

Special thanks to David Weiss and James McCorkle for their gentle wisdom and editorial care these past several years.

for Mary

TABLE OF CONTENTS

I

II

III

I

Uh-huh, I temped once. Temped a few weeks after college for a strange company. The company laminated cards. Laminated one type of card. The card had a button. There was a small button in the middle of it. In the middle of the card, but don't push it the foreman warned me. Don't push the button in the middle of the card the foreman insisted. What happens if I push it? I asked. I can't have been the first nor the only one to have asked what might happen. You're the first person to have asked that question said the foreman. That question simply isn't asked the foreman added. There were so many others laminating these cards and I was to believe that not one of them had asked why it is forbidden to push the button? And I'm to believe that not one of these people has asked this most obvious of questions? I asked the foreman. Perhaps in spite of your curiosity, once the card is laminated you are no longer forbidden to press the button. Once you laminate the card, you may press the button said the foreman. What do you mean the question isn't asked? I asked. How is such a state of affairs possible? I demanded of the foreman. I said you could press the button repeated the foreman. You may press the button into perpetuity, but it must first be laminated the foreman reiterated. I don't wish to press the button I replied to the foreman. Among the set of all pushable buttons there is not a single one I wish less to press I said to the foreman. My concern lies solely with the prohibition against pressing the button at the center of an erstwhile unlaminated card I assured the foreman. I'm sorry, but to answer your question would be to press the button on an as yet unlaminated card warned the foreman. If I were to address your concern, I would as well press the prohibited button elaborated the foreman. A notion which, as foreman, I am by definition unable to entertain. As foreman, I can only pretend never to have had this conversation the foreman concluded. This represents an imbroglio that would have been profitably avoided added the foreman and he walked away. Thank you I said to the foreman under my breath. Thank you for trellising the vines of my still vernal curiosity I told the foreman internally. One day I shall yield you an admirable vintage I promised the foreman *sotto voce*. And then I pressed the button and went to work.

The moment the initiate rushed in to announce that the mysteries had been parodied, a bird flew directly into the eye of one of the men assembled and was trapped inside his skull. Another man sitting to that man's right, who held the post of Quadrature, stood and exclaimed suddenly, "It always happens this way when the mysteries are parodied. A bird flies into a man's head, who has nothing whatsoever to do with the situation, and everyone is so surprised at this that the burlesque of the mysteries is forgotten. What was to be taken only as a *sign* of some tremendous outrage becomes the greater preoccupation." A third man, sitting well behind the rest of the assembly, rose and approached the first, thrust his hand into the mouth of the other and drew out the bird. With the bird in his hand this third man asked the Quadrature, "Is this always what happens next?" The other answered, "This is precisely what happens. A third man pulls the bird out through the mouth of the first and asks, 'Is this what happens next?'" "What, then, is going to happen next?" the third man asked. "Exactly," said the Quadrature, "That's always what follows." "Wait a minute," said the man clutching the bird, "How do we know you're not just watching what happens and then declaring that this is the way things always are?" "Why," asked the Quadrature, "would *you* wish to suggest that what has just happened isn't the way things always are?" "A bird just flew into my head," yelled the first man, "I for one have never heard of such a thing happening before." "And whose fault is that?" asked the Quadrature. "Will you dare lay the great weight of your own ignorance at *my* table?" "In all my life," insisted the man still holding the bird, "I have never, nor, I hazard, has anyone else here, heard of a bird flying into the skull of a man, and this with no apparent injury to the organs nested therein. I am a merchant, I am aware of prodigies both recent and ancient, and I can with justice claim that when a bird flies into the head of a man it may be accounted extraordinary." "Of course it's extraordinary, or else why would we take notice of it in the first place?" said the

Quadrature. "I may with equal justice claim that when a bird flies through the eye of a man and into his skull, people take immediate notice. What imbecility to witness such a sight and take it for a common occurrence . . ." "Oh shut up all of you!" the sergeant at arms screamed, "I know who profaned the mysteries! I can't stand to listen to any more of this. I am prepared to name names." "You are a liar," countered the Quadrature. "If you had only listened to me, I said that the profanation of the mysteries is always forgotten in the course of the ensuing astonishment at the flight of a bird into the first man's head." "But I'm telling you, I know who's responsible. I know for a fact that the mysteries were parodied." "You know nothing of the sort," declared the Quadrature. "The profanation of the mysteries must be forgotten in order for it to have happened," he insisted repeatedly until all the others fell silent in wonder and fatigue. "You all must forget the mysteries, and any profanation of them," he screamed. "You must forget all of it, or else justice shall never be done!"

how a pattern of (a.) violent
reciprocating ventures among enemies
giving way to (b.) dense rotarian
calms and (c.) back again, that is,
how, from (d.) continual interruptions,
to plot an (e.) uninterrupted trajectory
stands alone among (f.)
accomplishments as exemplary of (g.)
the totemistic headspace caught
boinking (h.) hot trophy wife of (i.)
imperialist justification, thus to
reinforce the (j.) *argumentum ad
pabulum* that (k.) sound government
"returns" to the "job" of (l.) "running
the country" as one would (m.) a
garbage disposal or (n.) sex toy, as if
to release the (o.) individual
consciousness to (p.) enjoy its attitude
toward history as a (q.) thing forever
passing into (r.) nothingness, since
whenever (s.) serious matters are
finally reduced to their (t.) non-serious
essence, and eunuchs are opening
splits of (u.) champagne and setting
out exotic cheeses, some (v.) buff
theory of time always rushes in to

announce that (w.) roving thugs have (x.) defaced the herms, and concluding with an (y.) accurate explanation of (z.) herms

Good afternoon. As you can see from the chart, two concentric ledges extend inward from the anterior surface of the upper skull, one slightly above the other, here and here, and along these ledges two animals move in opposite directions. Hence, we shall understand birth as a moment in time such that the counterclockwise-moving animal runs at infinite velocity, while the other's motion is so slow as to be indiscernible. Likewise, we shall define death as the converse, with regard to velocity, and conclude from these premises that you are able to understand what I am saying at this present moment only because the animals are moving at equal velocity. And now I'd be happy to field any questions you might . . . I said I'd be happy to . . . Hello?

It is difficult to resurrect the delicious, transitory sadness of the motel, because we rarely leave the motel in the first place. The motel is everywhere except for the place we consider the actual motel. The only actual thing in what we consider the actual motel is the loneliness we feel when we're there, so we actually leave the motel by staying in one from time to time. To sleep in a motel for no apparent reason resembles a tradition among family members of occasionally pretending they are not at all related. When the son arrives at his parents' door for Thanksgiving, he introduces himself as if he had never met them before and, smiling, asks if he might have a bit of their time. The parents are always very cordial. They ask him in, offer him a drink, invite him to stay for dinner, introduce him to his sister and brother-in-law and niece, who hands him a picture she's just finished drawing, that has his name written across the top of it. "Forgive her," the mother will say, "she still doesn't quite have the hang of it." The niece's apparent impertinence is another part of the tradition, as is the mother's apology. Anything that happens counter to the tradition preserves the tradition, the way sleeping preserves wakefulness, the way one can— by grinding a stone into dust, then coating each particle of that dust with a fine glue and reassembling those dust particles into a single slightly larger mass—accomplish what is usually dismissed as "softening a stone."

The musicians had begun to open their instrument cases and were stepping inside them as a bemused crowd gathered near about. They were stepping inside the cases to a depth that did not correspond either to the bottoms of the cases or to the ground beneath, for only the crowns of their heads were visible to the gathering numbers who watched, thinking this was some sort of magic show, and of course they could not help but clap and cheer when the right hand of each musician reached up to the lid of his case, pulled it shut and, as if by a mechanism hidden within, made all of the external clasps of the cases close together in perfect unison. When a group of men dressed in clothes identical to those of the musicians strode along and, without even coming to a full stop, reached down and took the cases by their handles and continued on their way, the crowd hesitantly approached those areas along the sidewalk where the cases had rested, searching for holes in the concrete where, so they were convinced, the musicians must still be hiding. Some began to stomp, others to jump up and down all about the two segments of concrete. A woman was heard to murmur to her friend, "Would that my husband, who is also a musician, and all his friends, were so easily disposed of." Those who were testing the solidity of the thoroughfare encouraged the standabouts to join in, holding out the possibility that a network of catacombs lay directly beneath their feet accessible by some weight-activated switch under the concrete slabs. By the time the perimeter in question had filled to capacity with every sort of jumping and stomping, another group of musicians had come along and, thinking these people in sore need of an accompaniment to their admittedly odd way of dancing, had taken out their instruments and promptly begun to play something they considered appropriate to the occasion. An elderly man, for whom stomping was a physical impossibility, yet hoping still to place himself in the service of the ensemble, knelt down slowly and placed his hat bottom up on the pavement in the event of some occasional gratuity. As soon as he had settled comfortably on a nearby bench, the sun, long hidden within a peninsular cloud, emerged from behind a crossing of migratory birds, capturing the attention of no one but a small child who, with emulative arms extended and head back, strayed from his mother's side into the noontime traffic.

THE SKEPTIC'S ANATOMICAL PARABLE OF SIGHT AS AN
INFINITE REGRESSION

Gatherers, or eaters, vintners, even sculptors, of light, they have been called, the eyes—lumenivores—sight, the *exquisite hunger of the self*—but these extravagant folkways, by an easy and rustic anatomy lesson, are quickly disposed of, for there is little to vision aside from a slab or great mortarwork stele (in *opus incertum*)—of tremendous height, I'll grant you—with fragments and powder of it broken and strewn at its base—thus the vaunted retina—Rome and ruin of the truth—and, for that matter, whether within or without the skull, what difference? A chauvinism merely, this within and without, the vulgar distinctions of a surveyor—yet, forced to conclude, let us with policy join the mob and situate it within, as the psychological epoch demands: that the matter be concluded *once and for all*, and that it be within, that the powers, the receiving powers, the individuating, sovereign element—to speak liberally, the sight—that in essence, all agencies of sense, of self-making, be located within, and, for the sake of brevity, and as not to importune the precious *untrammeled will*, perfect and absolute self, node of intention, governor, etc., we will, if only for the record, put the sight properly within the skull—with rudest carpentry house the jewel. Idiots!

In the lower interior reaches there stands in the dims and waste a witness, a groundling—vermin if it please you—squinting above him into the starless vault, following the stele heavenward as far as is visible, into, as the poets say, *shadows of neither evening nor unnatural day*, to a height at which one in dreams rises, but in waking associates with the unattainable, *close glooms of the upper skull*. From across a narrow chasm two portholes in horizontal attitude—oculi if you wish—of Leonardian circumference, bathe the empyrean reaches of our slab with the vague commotion of external fact and shed for our witness sufficient light to behold both a dense profusion of ivy growing along the illuminated face of the stele and one further marvel: hung, or in some manner suspended between access of light and immemorial brickwork, two spherical masses, half-illuminated, half nearly imperceptible. It is as accurately said that they float—a stationary hovering, two rippling moons, though, with adjustment to the dimness, it becomes plain to him rat-like below, that they are each a cloud, a swarm, a multitude of complementary and fleeting vectors spherically resultant—some, though never so many as to harm the collective endeavor, repairing to the ivy bower to roost and gender, some winging westward toward their extreme Gibraltar of light, but of what these trailing globes are composed the witness is always unsure. All that can be ascertained is the swarming, and that it kindles in him, who strains to see, the rudiments of his own attention. We might as well, for all the eyes may deduce, remove ourselves to his skull and find at its base, there among the broken stones and first shadows, another who stares above at the dim prodigy of two perfect but swimming spheres. Yet a third trepanation within the witness of the witness would only reveal the same composition—more witnesses, more steles, more spheres—always the unscalable monument, the silent watcher, always the scarcity of light and the inscrutable orbs before it—of birds perhaps, swallows to hazard a cleverness, viz. as of the light, a darting species to be approximate, birds at any rate, or possibly bats, and extraordinary darters those, offering over swallows the distinct advantage of such additional symmetry as to place vermin both above and below, a verminous antipodes, the self, or *batting about of light to ever more futile uses.*

addendum : Bats are not, properly, vermin.

The intruder is to be defined as one situated on his stomach, his wrists tied together behind his back, his chin wedged in a chock of wood or metal. All his body below the neck shall be housed, as by a carapace, in a close-built shelter—whether of wood or metal it makes little difference. At either side of his head, enormous paper cones shall be situated, the better to amplify the cries of gulls who, queued at the far end of the cones, form a line sufficiently straight to inspire wonder among any who happen by, whether man or gull.

Thus the intruder, in front of whom and slightly to his left a boy shall be posited who, with the intention of making it his target, shall place on the level stump of a tree a small medicinal bottle. In short order the boy's father shall emerge from out of a cottage to the intruder's right, yelling, above the din of the gulls, for the boy to come over to him. Neither boy nor gulls shall take notice, but rather continue, the boy his attempts to hit the bottle with stones, the gulls one after another mysteriously to air their grievances against the intruder. "Get over here, you little shit!" the father will, perforce, scream.

At this, the boy shall approach the bottle, take it in hand, and, with little preparatory fanfare, commence to insert it down into his own throat. Some too among the gulls shall take beak and head of another into their craws for a moment and then expel them, while yet others gather in a chorus formation near the boy and scream, but with no flapping of wings—this in a mild gesture of support.

The father shall, having viewed this spectacle with a mixture of disgust and sorrowful acknowledgement, after a moment turn and rush into the cottage. Upon reappearing he will have strapped to his head an elaborate apparatus of six caliper-like arms in the process of ratcheting open his mouth while a mechanism at its center begins—slowly at first and then at brief stages more swiftly—to insert an ancient bullet into his throat and then retract it, quickly and repeatedly. He shall, thus adorned, approach the choking boy and stand menacingly over him, who by this time should be in dire panic for lack of air. Nothing, however, in the way of acknowledgement shall pass between father and intruder, for what could more offend the intellect than such a rash commingling of categories?

To continue, the bullet shall be passing in and out of the father's throat with ever greater speed and depth, while gulls are compelled to light on his shoulders and fan their wings in such manner as to behood the father with a living headdress.

No sooner shall it be discovered by any who stand witness to these events than the absence of a mother shall be corrected by her Andromache-wild emergence from within the cottage. In an attitude of the Egyptian Nut, she shall kneel in a benevolent arch over the choking boy, her face directly across and mere inches away from the chock and cones, while her haunches rise toward the father, as if her dorsum were utterly indifferent to the original tenor of her intercessions.

A small fissure will then begin to open in the earth at the concealed feet of the intruder and the ground take hold of his ankles and at ever larger increments of his body take him down and push him back, removing him from the chock and returning him to it, until he at turns disappears entirely under the shelter and is again returned whence he had been only a moment before.

So it is that the father shall undress and kneel behind his wife and the earth suck down the intruder. In a strict train of thrusts, first of earth, then of father, the intruder's eyes shall meet the mother's but for a moment, and the gulls' deafening cry tear at his fleeting pleasure, and at turns, as our intruder is pulled again into his covert, there shall follow an opposing and, as it were, equilibratory incursion from the opposite direction, this one straight into the steadfast mother, who shall be likened in her soft-bodied mantling of the innocent to a gentle sky, and shall be made whole by her husband's ancient justice, suffering the harsh stroke of her domestic fate to force its way into her tenderness as she watches what could be hers withdraw, though she soon enjoy a momentary respite from cruel necessity as her hopes advance out of the darkness, and in so doing, lure—with the help of her husband, who himself is, it must be said, forced to swallow his own harsh fate, only to find he must swallow it again, and the intruder, let us not forgot the intruder—the tired, hesitant stars out of the refuge they are owed for all the turmoil created in their name.

The tinkling of filamental dust in a blown bulb would have been more audible than the voice of his youngest daughter, who, escorting me across the dining room to a niche in the wall where there lay an enameled bowl, whispered, "This is where we put the orchid blossoms after they've fallen off the stalk." They were, however, not blossoms at all, but rather the shed skins of miniature animals who appeared to have suffered terribly in their moulting.

"Why do you tell them they're orchids?" I asked her father later that night.

"You know, when I was younger," he said over his cognac, "I used to batten on such strange notions, that insects, for instance, must endure all those horrors of metamorphosis chiefly for my benefit, to add to my store of fine phrases—'tortured exuviae of the chitinous' comes immediately to mind. But that my love of phrases would keep me at a distance from—well, most everything else . . . for all my thinking, that's a notion I had never entertained until it was far too late. A long way around to say that if everything were swallowed up by orchids—you know, despite the depredations of collectors, it remains the largest family of flowering plants— let's say things could be far worse. I, though, shall never, no matter how hard I try, be swallowed up."

"But really," he continued after a moment, glancing at his daughters, "It's not so bad. Exile has plenty of meanings to keep one occupied, even this strange exile of mine, and I have only myself to blame for it. Anything, after all, can become an orchid, if you look at it long enough—"

"Anything can be anything."

That's not the way to open a garage door he yelled and took her by the hand to the attic insisted he was in truth a kind of fungus the human kind with little ceremony ripped off his pants revealed to her a supernumerary buttock and then another so forth until by summer the attic was fairly stuffed with them rafters strained to bursting a slight bulge at the soffits one shingle then another falling into the mock orange and hosta girdling the breezeway below so the children disguised themselves as thoroughly as to provoke a fear in others they themselves could not begin to understand even if that beginning lay in an innocent application of paints and the panicking guards they dealt their heavily sleeved blows to the oils the powdered bismuthic hues and codling moth binders the children concocted these with no assistance but the wild stochastic vindictiveness of possibility and with equal vindictiveness as their excitement crested the paints found a way into their pores according to their unwitting chemic facility the more the guards beat them the truer the disguise became the guards' beating them especially so under a sun shining without blemish confounded the real and the play disguise and disguised into an undifferentiated mass of perfect light that of course the guards beat them they were guards after all who else were they going to beat

In a well-lighted central corridor she stopped me abruptly and with great insistence said she did not know me, an absurdity which, under most circumstances, would have struck me as utterly delightful. In this case, though, I found myself overtaken by an almost aggressive perplexity, for in fact not two weeks prior at the party of a friend I had made this very woman's acquaintance.

"You're quite mistaken," I said to her, "Do you not remember the party at H's just recently?"

"I am insulted that you would think to associate me with such a person, sir!"

"But . . . he is not widely known. I am confused. Do you deny having been at the party at all?"

"Who are you to examine *me* this way, especially in view of the certainty that I am not the least acquainted with you, not in any way."

"Who am *I*? May I remind *you* that it was you who stopped me?"

"Impelled by a necessity I feel it hardly my obligation to explain to you, sir. Suffice to say, I do not know you."

"Far be it from me, strange woman, to feel any greater obligation to inform you how bizarre it appears to accost someone in the public thoroughfares only to make the singularly useless claim that you are ignorant of his existence. What—do you mean to take me into your glittering eye by these spells of absurdity? Will you tell me *eftsoons* some tale of great import involving pack ice and talismanic birds?"

As if by the force of my satire, the features of her face began to smooth and draw themselves into longitudinal seams, by which barricading exertions her hair appeared simultaneously to be pulled down into the body of what, I was certain, would soon open into a perfect tulip. She turned and walked away in the direction whence she had approached me, content, I suppose, that she had laid waste to both my mockery and my certitude. At some twenty paces she turned again, and—the audacity of the woman—quite suddenly allowed the tulip head to open, then lifted her arms and tapped each of the petals one by one, only as hard as was required to break them at their base, as if to suggest that this lack of effort stood in wildly inverse proportion to what she felt was due me by way of retribution, that the bones of all my memories lay wrapped in fat within that efflorescence, an imposture of sacrifice at last exposed.

For a time the *spoon man* knew his hare lip only as "Gervaise," but now his body lay in a culvert. To nearly all who knew him, he was the *spoon man*, or if the desire were to show an easy intimacy, simply *spoons*. Often he would pretend that one or the other of his hands was a fish, a transparent fish, and when he moved the hand slowly in front of his face, moving it as a fish would move, he would assure whomever happened to be looking that they could still see that part of his face obscured by his hand. To his hare lip he would say, "Gervaise, only through the lens of this merciful fish will he find you who can explain your terrible beauty to me, but is it not strange that to talk to you requires that you talk to yourself? Where is the meaning in this?" Yet a man whose head was shaved all but for six dots at the base of his skull began to repeat to his wife, "I told you, it's the *spoon man*, the *spoon man's* body lies in the culvert, and no one will claim it. This shall become one of our great enigmas. Yes, years hence, boys shall build fires and roast the spitted hare and repeat the tale of the *spoon man's* body." In the midst of such obsessions, is it surprising he should find solace in chewing upon his lip until it were divided, and his wife in horror cry, "You, you are the *spoon man*! Oh, the butchery of it!"

A Caribbean man playing peekaboo with a film student from behind the sandwich counter of a convenience mart let his jaw drop so low in playful enthusiasm that it looked to the student as though the great Odessa staircase had suddenly taken the place of his dentition.

"What on earth," you will ask, "has the depth to which the man dropped his jaw have to do with the appearance of his teeth?" fully expecting me to pull out some manner of baseless tinker tale about how, should the jaw be so off-puttingly lowered as to stand at near orthogonals to a plane described by the tips of the upper teeth, risers and treads shall suddenly extend from both sides of the inferior maxillary according to an hermetic-magical physiology of extreme dislocations.

But neither shall I explain away the student's hallucination (except to say that the Carib *had* opened his mouth, and to considerable dimensions, as part of the composite masquerade of astonishment one must affect in the game of peekaboo, and that he *had* covered his eyes with his hands, making it that much easier for the student to dissociate the gaping mouth from its physiognomic context and take it at first for an elevated grot, with a priest or two climbing along twin marble defiles on either side toward the soft, stalactical uvula), nor otherwise diminish the source of his terror upon seeing in flight up those now gleaming *gradûs ad nusquam* both of his parents, cloaked and glancing nervously behind them as if in the direction of some murderous pursuer.

By how much the student's terror swelled as soon as he realized those glances were directed at *him* one could measure only by the subtlest tremor along his eyelids and a slight whitening at the knuckles as he dug his fingernails under a strip of chrome flashing that extended from one end to the other of the delicatessen case. "I am powerless to save them. They will surely fall to their deaths. Those are, after all, the Odessa steps, and I am a fool for having thought it so!" "I am powerless, powerless!" he was screaming at the Caribbean man, who had, with considerable alarm, taken his hands from his eyes and quickly closed his mouth. Unhappily for him, at precisely this moment, he discovered a small particle of food wedged in a crevice between two of his lower teeth and absently, while staring in amazement at the student, attempted to dislodge it with his tongue. The sight of that brief protrusion just beneath the Carib's lower lip sent the student lunging over the sandwich counter, screaming, "My parents, no, let them alone, they mean nothing to you!"

but never *Quite,* follows *Quite* into bar saying, "I'm *Not Quite,* following you." *Quite,* nervous, holds his money close to his genitals. But *Not Quite,* close enough to see it, asks *Quite* loudly, "Am I *Not Quite,* able to see your money close to your genitals? Sure I am!" And *Quite,* liable now to run away with his money near his genitals; *Not Quite* to his left, so down stairs to the right, *Not Quite* on his heels, running after him asking, "Did he go that way? because I'm *Not Quite,* sure that he didn't go this." Far into the cellar now, *Quite,* but *Not Quite* down far enough to yell to him, "*Quite,* alone you are, and ever shall be as long as I'm *Not Quite,* following you, *Quite,* to the end of what said *Quite,* naturally holding his money close to his genitals, would call his life!"

Indeed what I said to him—not knowing for sure whether I had the right man or not—and he couldn't have misheard me, it was too early in the day for that—least of all for him, who was *as incapable of error as stone,* or so he once characterized himself to someone he might have thought was me—though admittedly I would have as soon run away with my hands over my ears had I met with such a quiddity as I presented to him, but he didn't, which convinces me afresh that he heard exactly what I told him, and what's more, by staying on as he did, only proves that he *was* the man, and, more importantly, that he had *already heard these words* and was, as I said, staying on not out of politeness as much as perversely to confirm that these words were being said *once again,* and even more perversely, to *him,* rather than, as so long ago in this very park, to another, while he looked on, helpless against their effect, as they went so quickly to work, these very same words, on, as it happened, his wife, who, so she had previously boasted, was possessed of an *independent mind,* and he looking on, watching in utter amazement as these words—which until this morning he was certain he would never hear again, *even if they should be spoken to him,* even if everyone in the immediate area should hear them as clearly as he, for he would have girded himself against the statistically impossible event that their combination might once again approach his ears, he would have lived in such a way as to negate the very possibility of their utterance—watching, as I say, as his *independent-minded* wife felt the strength quite disappear from her legs upon hearing what I repeated to him again this morning, and one may fairly guess that he succeeded in conducting himself afterwards according to a single purpose, which was to live as to avoid ever again hearing those words, until now—seeing that they had convinced his wife so many years before that her bones were *made of air,* and she did suddenly, to his horror, fall to the ground in a heap that day (not that I was in any way surprised, it having been proved to me beyond doubt that to bring about a physiological *peripeteia* in one as *teeteringly proud* as she, one had only to speak the truth)—for he stood perfectly still after, as I say, an unimpeded audition of the words, so still, in fact, and for such duration—at this present writing he remains immobile—as to be mistaken for stone, which, of course, settled it for me, even if I should admit that I had never seen him in motion.

A half-headed woman entered the loge walking backwards. "These times are a feral mud horse, yet you just cook away up here in your twee decency," she declaimed to the occupants of the loge. Her head, halved longitudinally, betrayed no sign of having suffered wedge or blade-borne violence; along the revealed, once interior surface, in a diagonal course from the upper left– to lower right–hand corner, the principal episodes of her life were minutely sculpted in a bas-relief that, raised along the cross-section of variegated tissues, effected a transparent mirage, as of a summer's roadway horizon scrummed by radiant heat. "An untamed mud horse are these contemporary times," she reiterated more softly and with the inflections of one attempting to convince herself of the truth of a propagandistic slogan. The men and women in the loge meanwhile were finding it more difficult to avoid the conclusion that she had dreamt them into existence, anything to siphon off the abstraction of minds other than her own there in the intruded loge. "My halved head, *lllllook* at it," she ordered them. Curiously, for her to draw out the liquid consonant required that she afterward very quickly murmur, in an expiative tone serving to address some obscure grievance, a litany of identities, coeval and reassuring: "I am Cake Pang Dong, I am Easy NyQuil, I am Washable Nadine, etc." This pungent clamor soon broke free from the strict courtesies of the loge for all in the theater to hear. "Nighttime in this loge is damp beyond use," she yelled toward the stage. "We're calling an evening in this loge nothing but some damp money, do you hear?" and quickly thereafter, *sotto voce*, "I am the Saturationist, I am Flying W, I am My Own Personal Stalin, etc." The collective attention could be espied shifting like pooled fur away from the bandaged wilds of the proscenium toward her lips, which in profile flared with transverse riot against the private thunder of her halved head, suggestive of other, more violent involvements and litanies, other loges. "You want I give *you* the half-headed experience?" she threatened, turning her attention once again to those nearest her, "you want I *excuuuuse* half the legislators in your statehouse, see how you like it? Huh?" and then softly to herself, "I am Deep Chrysler, I am Cauterize That, I am *Ars Combinatoria*, etc." But the women among them there in the loge, though they still hung fearfully inside their black finery, had begun to take an interest in her vulnerable ferocity, tracing occasionally with furtive index the plane of the *norma mediana*. "No, of course not, you're all bleeders," she sneered, but then, as if drawing a needful supplement of oxygen from a source somewhere on her person, she turned aside and breathlessly intoned, "I am Gel Cap *Sang-Froid*, I am Grown Lax with Intermingled Norms, I am The Other Kind of Penis, etc." The longer she remained in the loge, the more completely all its occupants, man and woman, were assimilated to the portico of her hemicranial passion, which they began in their minds to liken to a treatment by Piranese, to the bleaching by time of the Parthenon, the Venusian dismemberment, but it was their growing ease with a half-headed woman taking by siegecraft their very exclusive coigne that suggested that a yet more stylized ruination had begun to envine the expectant, classical motifs that bordered and veined loge, lord, and lady alike. "I'll tell you what, I have *had* it with all you pathetic bleeders. I have crossed a Montaigne threshold, people," she yelled at the now smiling patrons. "A Montaigne threshold, do you hear me," and she too was smiling. "My casual, large-spirited, and explicative *bonhomie* has become as a poison to—" and by the catch in her voice, they were now bold enough to add in monotone, *mezzo piano*, "You are the Boo-Jet Theresa, you are Have a Mood On, you are Swastikas for Toes, etc."

Count the number of people you have touched and write that figure in the space provided.

> Do you mean the number of people upon whom I have laid a hand, or rather those whom I have "affected" through some non-tactile sort of communication, or the sum of these?

We are asking that you count the number of people you have touched over the years who, if queried, would reply, *Yes, that person touched me*—however one might understand the word—and to write that number in the space provided.

> So what you are asking me is approximately how many people would respond, in such manner as you would safely deem credible, that, indeed, I had served as the active agent of the "palpatation" in question, whether tactile or other?

We are asking you to write in the space provided to the nearest whole digit, the number of people who, when asked, *Did he touch you?* would respond, *Yes, there was a time when I thought of myself as having been touched by him.*

> And by this I assume you mean to ask how many people can remember a period in the past when, if asked, *Who are you?* would reply definitively, *I am one whom he* (viz. me) *has touched*—and that regardless whether the contact was physical or conative?

We are asking you merely to think back in time, as it is said, to all those you have known who at one time or another found themselves in a position to say, when asked quite anonymously whether or not you had touched him or her: *I seem to recollect my having entertained once a frame of mind in which to be touched by him meant that "I was,"* and to write the number of those thus described in the space provided.

So that I understand you fully, you are asking me to count the number of people who were once in a position to remember themselves as such as could describe their state of mind during the period in question as one of preparing to accept that, upon reflection, they had once been touched by me, whether in flesh or spirit, suchwise that their own existence was therein revealed to them, and to admit that to impersonal query?

We are simply asking, in accordance with standards of procedure long established, that you recall, with as much accuracy as you deem within your present powers, the number of people who, when asked, *Did he touch you?* would reply, *Yes, under present circumstances, it lies within the tolerances of accuracy for me to characterize an understanding of at least one among various former "conditions" in my long life as having been in some manner or other touched by him, such that, if asked whether this recollection was the sole means by which any self-understanding were at all possible during or around the time either of the initial contact or the recollection thereof, regardless whether I am CURRENTLY willing to offer any credence to this characterization . . . I could comfortably aver,* and write that number legibly in the space provided.

Just in case I've misconstrued, you're asking me to . . . .
. . . .
. . . .
. . . .
. . . .

. . . .
. . . .
. . . .
. . . .
. . . .
. . . .
. . . .
. . . .
. . . .
. . . .
. . . .
. . . .
. . . .
. . . .
. . . .
. . . .
. . . .
. . . .
. . . . : ——————————————— .

(space provided)

33

Glistening shank of the bully in hoist. Rakers in dawn procession. Tattoo of their stark cadence from filleted tambours. Shadow of pendant bullyshank shifting in swing over the Ambit. Rakers commencing their rite. Pale gravel, a hiss between tines. Cereal passivity of stone.

Lower the bullypart then, they at the tackle. At increments, the hallowed lowering. Circular Ambit of gravel beneath, windlass at the marge. Temenos of gravel. Undulatory, those furrows. Rakers to their dance amid solemn lays intoned at the marge. Gentle subsidence of stone under shankload at touchpoints.

When finally the shank at rest and the taut harness slackened, rakers removed to the marge, to the benches. Antiphonal chorus of lays redoubled, rakers to the weedy bounds. The furrowed circle clear. Tackle squad absorbed in minute adjustment of shank as to position. Rakers at periphery pulling at weeds, inattentive.

Gathering of flies amid debate as to position. Among tackle squad, furtive wavings away of flies, incorporate decorum. Sequent chuckle among those trained at the benches. Quiet disputes around the teeming shank. Many frustrate swipes at carnivorous flies.

General discomfiture, laymen in gradual egress for the noon tea. Slim rillet of putrefaction ascending godward. Delicate furrows of stone amid waxing debate abolished under sandal. With consensual gravity among the tackle squad, lyes laid unto the shank. Barrows of lye at lee edge of Ambit. Shank laid into with cutlery and lyes.

Westward garland of cloud foretelling nightfall. At abatement of shank teemings, pride of the tackle squad. Surcease of levity among the benches. Pocket torches and cigarettes now the rakers' burden. Insolent tuning of radios, a spreading of blankets. Vapor rillet brushing the godhead's sinus. Soporific oblivion among the divine host to the compressed lyes. Interval of disquiet around the shankcarcass. Nervous but determined solemnity at shankside. Their close shave with the spoiler flies.

Raker host in slow dispersal for evening mess. Languid tugs at the bedclothes among the deities turning in slumber. Goddess chafing in her teddy. Importunate friction of lace. Untoward anecdotes circulating then among the tackle squad in casual transit toward barracks. At increments more savagely, the bully's life lampooned.

Midnight. Bloody Sarum of gravel. Mess of the shank moistening at dewfall.

Hemorrhaging emotionally whenever I heard the song, "Old Folks" (although the therapist pleaded, in her most unfortunate phrases, that I *focus* on how I was too young to have the same kind of *connection* to the melody that an older person—who had "experienced *the war* and *objective, societally-based obstructions to a natural sense of sexual freedom*"—might), I would want to peel in haste a square of skin of very specific dimensions away from the part of my body "it had striven to protect" (according to the judicious construction she had put on my previous attempts at a less considered, spontaneous *écorché*) and prop the flap of it up with toothpicks, or lacking those, suffer to resort to cotton swabs, which, with their softer termini, would barely suffice as standards for this sheltering "flag of my dysposition," torn (so she was determined to convince me) from "the one remaining garment I could consider safe from adulteration" (which finally proved her utter uselessness, as I had long before come to regard the skin as, beyond doubt, a *treacherous Nessus robe*), and underneath it sit in the rain of my Dis-embodied attitudes to sing "Old Folks" repeatedly, for sooner or later they must rise, those shades—of men who had been women and of great warriors—from the Acheron I had every reason to hope would turn up in the course of these my excavations, carried forth with neither map nor bough of gold, and when they had departed, those impetuous impotent dead, I would, disburdened, leave off with razor and song, but not without much sadness, for a proper man must betimes go a flensing, if not the shoulder of a whale, why then that of his own shall do, to release the dead trapped thereunder. There are always dead thereunder.

demand also   this night   they be carried on palanquins   by us remaining

to the walls   damnable mimicry of our   sacred triumphs

where must erect their "trophies"   prevailed upon me to relinquish scepter

topped off with   severed wolfsnout   see it now

raised above their effeminate banners and fans   have come up short

not to have foreseen   these late invasions   in past   seized anyone

found above a mile   within borders   find fault in no one but my

the informants   they must have cozened   her attendants

our late queen   though of course   her foetus

quite dead for lack of   certain necessary   instruments

"Principiis obsta," they jeered   fell from her pubis into basket

placed below her   did suspend   the "offending" mother

in leather sling   with "committee members"   in chairs

repeated their overtures to her   as to giving forward the child

it was fathered by   bless her   refusing to explain

"the worm"   gotten in her   though they at turns

with mock reverence   her grace as "womb" of state   "unconverted center

of foul pulsations"   is a method they have

our vanquishers   deprives enemies of all sensation   by sharpened shell

scaphopod mollusk   found hereabout   toothshell they say charmingly

pushed to its length   up nasal fossae

quite undoes one   beautiful   the ingenuity of it

They came then calling themselves *the Gate*, and told of their birth from out of a deposit of metal under the ground and demanded that we recognize them as superior. For our languors and bandling stupidities and hesitation to pay them this honor, *the Gate* soon brought on that it had been from a *lustrous* metal that they arose, as when a thing said to be *shiny* awakens the listener, and no reflective surface in sight, so that to say *shiny* is literally to shine, and awakens the eyes, an effect of little notice in these days warm now in our mutual noon of steel and mirrors, but it was *the Gate* first shone using the word *shiny*, so *the Gate* was the beginning, to whom it had fallen by extraordinary lot they must enter the narrows of this world as from a sowing of teeth into the womb below full of *lustrous* metal to bring an end to those dimensionless nights under the earth, as it has since been said of our own meaningless endurance before their arrival when a *gens* broke forth in gleams consundered from the earth and its damp assumptions. "We are *the Gate*," they said. "You may now ask," they told us, "around whose fist your hair is wound when we pull back your head and your neck bends like a leaf against the squall. It shall remain our fist, but you may ask and this shall be a milk to you." "Treat of the weapon to cure the wound, cauterize the channels that deliver confusions, we are *the Gate*," they said. "Who lifts dull suns to low noons," warned *the Gate*, "will drown them in the dusk of an incontinent lap and pass out of this world." "Here now, out of your uteri and wooden money—come, enter *the Gate*. Take the whole carcass of your here-I-am and destroy it to good purpose, else how to consider your blood as anything more than a style of communication between diffident substances? What are you afraid of? These are only words, all except one: *Gate*." "Speak often and squander your credit," said *the Gate*, "speak seldom and the spurned word hurls itself upon you like a suicide." "You are now in the hand of *the Gate*, the new hand. Came into your little room a torrid zone of truculent want in the form of a hand, and forced your chin up unnaturally, and you liked it. So you thought you were waiting for a different hand?" Came *the Gate*.

As for how long I had been sleeping out in the open I could not say, nor explain how I might have been removed to such a place without my knowledge, but I awoke soon enough with a crowd gathered thereabout in sufficient numbers that I could with good reason yell "Disperse immediately!" and "There's nothing to see here, please move on!" and "Give her room!"—all sorts of public imperatives I had neither the pleasure nor the permission ever, as child or anti-child, to say aloud. And they obliged me too, the crowd, yet not by stepping back or walking away but rather in moving, many with their arms outstretched, closer and closer, as though "to disperse" had provisionally come to mean its opposite, and to call them "them" to disown *myself* in the coldest of terms, for I lay back down in a wadi of bruised linen, the better to encourage their soft inevitable ingress into my, well, body, for lack of knowing just what sort of receptacle I had become that could accommodate such a tribute, and fashioned from their quiet entry into me a silent steady motion of cloud trains that would pass, like the locomotion of successive centuries, far overhead, above the shimmer of sunlight among trembling fascicles of pine needles, with the distinct effect of putting me back indoors, where so little can happen to one who will, with no effort of her own, routinely awaken in a busy open-air market to the tightening curiosity of crowds.

I.

The boat was moored in a cove. Mother and father had gone ashore and left my sister and me on board to wash the decks. One of them had thrown a kerosene lamp. We were rinsing down the cockpit when both of us saw a woman rowing very quietly in an old dinghy away from a clump of junipers. My sister climbed to the mast and held the halyards away from it and asked if I could hear a faint metallic clicking. "A little," I said. We tried to look busy when the stranger pulled up alongside and drew in her oars. My sister said hello. The woman was very old and wore a torn blue scarf, the corners of which were drawn together under her chin with a gold ring. There was a strange wrinkle above her upper lip. One of her eyes was clouded over. On the forward thwart of the dinghy there was arrayed, all open and playing, a row of music boxes, more than twenty. Some were made of wood, others covered with satin. One had a blindfolded ballerina turning in its center. When her oars were stowed, she pulled two large waterfowl from the bottom of the dinghy, one in each hand, and stood up and asked us, "Which of these is your father?" "My father is a man," I said to her. "He will be," said my sister.

II.

"If the stars fall, will they burn through the sails?" I asked my sister. Mother and father were asleep below. It was one o'clock in the morning. By compass we sailed on a following wind around the shoals known as Cross of Mouths in a curve whose name we could not pronounce, though we knew it to be infinitely long. Orange and red panels of the spinnaker through which the moon shone cast across the deck a color we knew only as "one o'clock and nearing the Cross of Mouths." When we passed into the broad shipping channels, my sister reached inside the companion way and switched off the running lights. Soon we were hedged round by limitless banks of cold and time. The warmth of our passage through them felt like the trail left by a half- articulated question. Later in the night, leaves began to fall on the decks and into the water on either side of the boat, maple leaves, illuminated by moonlight as they fell out of their darkness. We were hours beyond sight of shore. "But where are the trees?" I asked my sister. "These leaves are real," she said without looking up from the compass. The light of the binnacle threw her eyes into shadow. "These are the only true leaves there could ever be."

III.

It was late March. The boat was up in its cradle. One half of the bottom had been sanded for painting. On the other half, my sister and I drew pictures with chalk. She drew horses, many of them, all from the same angle. I put plus signs between the horses and then drew an equals sign after the fifth horse and then a boat. We both laughed. She drew a boat under a division bar and a snake to the left. "Vessel divided by snake equals . . ." "Mom," I said, and we laughed even louder. We played catch with a tie-dye colored kick ball. A tall man we didn't know with one leg shorter than the other came up and wanted to see it. My sister looked over at me then turned to give it to him. He snatched it out of her hands and held it out away from his face. He looked at it and looked at it. We grew frightened. Suddenly he spat to his side and yelled, "This ball curdles my blood," and hurled it over my head and turned and limped toward a station wagon where a woman waited. She was waving to me and pointing in the direction the man had thrown the ball. When they drove away, I turned and went to look for it. I walked into a large patch of wild carrot between two immense and aged cabin cruisers rotting away in their cradles. It was like entering a gorge to go between them. In the shadows I parted the wild carrot and tall grass. I found half a ladder and an old block with cracked wooden cheeks and sheaves rusted in the swallow. The hulls of the cruisers curved and rose over my head. There were flies. I slapped one hull and stepped sideways and slapped the other. Under the rusting screw of one of the hulls, there lay, half in sun, half in shadow, a dead deer. Someone had cut an elaborate flower shape out of a newspaper ad for boys' clothing and then cut a circle out of the flower's center and placed it over the eye of the deer. Rain had molded the paper to the shape of the deer's head. Dimes were inserted between the lips of the deer in such a way that the dimes looked like teeth. I flecked maroon paint from the bottom of one of the cruisers as I stared at all this. Chips of paint fell onto the deer's haunches. My sister came up from behind and was silent. After a time I kicked the deer hard. One of the dimes fell out of its mouth. My sister said, "Did you just kick the deer?" "You *saw* me kick it," I said. "That's why I asked," said my sister.

IV.

I had not yet finished dressing and already too many people were streaming into the house. I knew this without leaving my room. When I ran to the top of the staircase, my sister was already there. She had made a pouch for her shell collection by gathering up her nightgown in the front. One of her arms was through the sleeve of a sweater. The rest she was pulling over her torso as though readying to leave. "You people look too much like fire coming into the house like that," she said to them, though they gave no indication that they heard her. The sound of her voice reminded me of a marble we had buried near the river, thinking it looked too much like an eye. I ran back to my room and took down the poster of North American freshwater fishes and rolled it up and put on my sneakers. There wasn't time to look for the last thing. When I came back to the stairs, my sister had her sweater all the way on. The shells were arranged in a perfect square on the floor, and she stood within it looking out of a window toward the bay. I told her I was ready to go. "We're already there," she said.

I was taught that the shape of a body lives longer than a body itself. Likewise, I was taught to build at the shore, when the disfigurement of living was complete, whether from age or disappointment, a simple enclosure. I built mine of bleached drift and rootwood near where a newly risen stream gave out into the lake. Syringes and tampons shifted in among the leaf-litter at its bottom, darkened in patches by the shade of sumacs growing along its banks. I pulled up the roots that ran into deeper water and cut through them with half a scissors. My hand bled as I bound the drift with the root, and there was a willow over me whose eye I caught unraveling in a bee. As I walked to the store to buy lard, I thought of what it would be like to walk inside a bee. When I brought the lard to the counter, the grocer was staring at me. "God help us," he said as he passed the canisters over the scanner. "Yes, them too," I said, and gathered up the lard.

Since I was borne out of the only place into this one, I pissed all over the enclosure and then plastered the interior with lard. It was very hot the day I went for good into the enclosure. There were cones under my face that had begun to drill toward a mussel somewhere in deep. For most, the enclosure would have looked like an unreadable letter until I crawled into it. Of course, once inside and no longer able to distinguish where my skin ended and the lard began, and after that, what was lard and what stick, it became readable enough for a boy and a girl to come up to the side of the enclosure and for the girl to say, "I'm going to touch the christ child."

"Mom said not to touch the christ child," said the boy. "She said not to *trust* the christ child, so I'm going to touch it instead," and she put her hands against the enclosure. I could feel my eyes growing too far distant from one another ever to be considered a pair again.

as his mother—a perfect question mark in white smoke—was fond of saying: he had but to stride into the enemy village, surely *that* lay within his competence, and on no pretext whatsoever, would convince them that he—not his physical presence so much, nor especially his "spirit," but more the *idea* of him (appealing, as one might expect, to their understandable provincialism, given their remarkable isolation, the lack of astronomy, of a sky, for that matter)—he was such as could, merely by entering a village, turn things about so, who could march right in, "just like that," as his mother—a lamp-lit region bordered on either side by cypress boughs—was frequently heard to say, and present himself with such force of character as to allow them to divine for themselves, *for themselves mind you!* the letter that would complete their alphabet, and to bring this immortality onto himself not by argumentation, that would have sullied the majesty of the deed—syllogisms, hugger-mugger premises slipped in by the cryptoporticus, no indeed—but just by his pure, unstudied saunter into their village, and that almost feminine insolence in the curl of his mouth, as if by an overdeveloped philtrum, the upper lip pulled toward the nose and thereby plumped at its hunkers, which upon phonation, would give at one and the same moment shape and sound to their missing—here, do you have a napkin, I'll draw it for you, it's a perfect match for his profile, from the good side, that is—the capstone to their alphabet that they'd sought nigh since "the teethings of Methusaleh," a phrase his mother—that thought experiment left out in the rain to rust—claims to have coined, that he was the very sign for which their oracles would keep watch, why, the *sign of a sign*, and yes, his mother—a contrivance laid aside by the age of miracles—would soon assure me, of course a lip has hunkers, every element of the physiology represents a miniature of the whole, the ear has its eyes and the eyes a belly—that never fills, be sure of that—as she once remarked—and thus would her son read the annals of his own birth, triumph, and heroic death in a single letter of his own unintended fashioning, and who could claim a like achievement, since the enemy would never reveal the inspiration, would adduce some Cadmus or Thoth, as if the names of letters really once were the names for things, uh-huh, wink-wink, oh yes, an aleph is an ox, I'm sure, *and my son is a zed*, or something of the sort his mother—the lost father who, recovered from a block of ice, resumed his life among the living as a woman—told me after her son's funeral, he who had never left the house and died, as she said under her breath, from a fall in the shower.

He had brought out a length of velvet suspended on a drying wicker and began to address it as "poor James." "*What, what say you, James, do speak up.*" "By moving one's finger north along poor James here, north meaning up and out, out there— look, do you see—" and he pointed with great intensity toward some constellation of fiery bodies of his own devising.

"My motive in bringing forth poor James? Well I can assure you, I have no intentions of inflicting another damnable golem on the world. They're all the rage, it would seem . . . I have it in mind, in fact, to prove that the world itself is a golem, *the* golem. There can only at all times be one and only one golem. In truth, I thought it might be *me*, until the blessed accession of our poor James convinced me of the *golemite condition of this world*"—and his mechanical genius but a length of fabric, with a nap that trended southward.

"Of course there's no use in explaining oneself, using numbers to account for numbers, that sort of incestuous calculation, you know, bumbershoots and all that, hip-hip, as they used to say, but it is the tissue of that very failure, that singular incapacity to explain oneself—as well to oneself as to another—that brings us round to poor James here, for that failure is the very *consciousness*, you see, breaking forward out of an inertial morass of, oh, how do you say . . . of involuntary preoccupations: cleaning the animal, keeping it warm and whole, or whole-ish at least—'the figure in the carpet' as someone once remarked—his name escapes me at the moment."

Until the commencement of this earnest demonstration, his dinner guest's every movement, as he described them later, had seemed of the unambiguous, "Please, help yourself" variety, but upon his bringing out poor James she ceased paying him any attention, and left abruptly, before the meniscus of her brandy had even yet resolved to the horizontal. Several of his friends at the club, upon hearing of these misadventures, and in possession of some prior knowledge concerning the woman in question, made jokes to the effect that it would never be discovered, the precise location of her genitalia, velvet golem or no, that her legendary clitoris lay stashed away in some Khyber Pass of affective remoteness she was apt to inflict in extra measure on one as gone-and-the-Lord-Chestnut-be-damned as he . . . and his ridiculous "poor James." "Ponder the possibility that perhaps she meant, 'By all means, save yourself,'" one of them suggested. "She plays in a string quartet," another observed. "Good night! How much louder must the warning siren sound?" a third expostulated from across the table. "Read the pattern in your little carpet, old man!"

Oh, but he smarted at this last jibe, for it had been uttered with no consideration for his protégé, upon whom—draped there along the wicker beside him steadfast and quiet for the length of their first luncheon together—he had trained his dearest hopes.

To the immediate right of a urinal I happened once to be using, a gentleman had oriented the grille on the vent nozzle of a hand dryer in such a way that, with each supination of his palms, I could feel slight gusts brush over the exposed portion of my calf beneath the grey sheet metal partition. By some freak of serendipity, it so happened that these intermittent gusts were distributed over time in perfect accord with the rhythmic pattern of the imbecilic old Juan Tizol chestnut, "Perdido," and, by clocking in at an extreme *Lento* that approached, by my wholly reliable inner metronome, a mere twenty beats per second, only served to fortify my surmise that strange, unsuspected periodicities not only garnish but add to experience that irreducible savor of uniqueness by which the sensorium, without any conscious effort on our part, deduces the uni-directional flow of time. So it was that the near imperceptibility of this particular occasion, compounded by the miracle of its occurring twice in succession—which I suppose would have been necessary in any case for me to recognize the pattern—impelled me, against all better judgement, to announce as much to everyone else in the lavatory, for however alert I have been to peculiar simultaneities or rhythmic consonances of one sort or another,* I have never sufficiently appreciated the profit that comes of keeping one's private revelations on a short leash.

Oh, the beating I took that night, though with the remarkable feature that the resulting bruises on my forearms and thighs, when brought into a particular conjunction, described almost exactly the shape of the Empire of Trebizond along the southern Euxine just prior to the Seljuk incursion of 1214.

---

*Once, many years ago, for instance, while driving, I arrived at an intersection behind an Oldsmobile Cutlass Supreme (again the memory lies quite beyond reach of any effacing power) to find that our directional signals were flashing at the rhythmic ratio of 2:3 (two of mine to every three of his), known to musicians as hemiola, which they, and perhaps others too (though I have never had occasion to bring it up with any but musicians) insist on pronouncing as if the "e" were long, as in "beet," leading me to assume incorrectly for years that the word derived somehow or other from the Greek for blood (αιμα)—whence are derived such useful terms as "haemophilia" and "haematoma"—with the result that I spent many unrecuperable hours entertaining all sorts of ill-founded notions (for the hemi- in hemiola signifies, quite obviously, half) of how certain folk dance rhythms I happened to be studying at the time were based on the cardiac cycle.

The csárdás becomes an irregular complex of musical phrases, a phrase village . . .
—*T. Adorno on Bartok's 3rd String Quartet*

Down by the bickering Pal I heard men fighting. I hummed to myself, *"The graph saves a dweeb."* I hummed to myself, *"The graph saves a . . ."* Hummed, *"Heigh-ho the merry . . ."* I said to myself, "Pinkl's been fingered, be off, be off!" Of course, the elusive "said to myself" without my having to saying so. "That's 'say so,'" she said, pinned to the then and there like a moth behind glass, but didn't know it. The way I don't know you: a little pasty . . . no, a little clunky.

"Yet," I conjectured to myself, "what is the ratio of paradise to mud?" And the near shore was turbulent with fish. The bickering, turbulent Pal. Let's assume I heard men fighting. "The hake is bad," she told me, "and so much floats along, buoyed by our faults." She wanted to join the FBI. Over a plate of venison. She wanted to confess. "Do it," I said, ". . . now!" "Hey, Qleo" I said (I was busy), "what's in the bag?" "Men fighting," he said. "I assumed as much," I said, and showed him my rubber spinach. "That's so cool," said Qleo. The police were but a thin film of worry over his ambitions. "I need to make water into a violin," said Qleo, "while the strapless night still preens itself . . ." ". . . in the fender of Hathor's Nova . . ." I could finish *anything*. After a swim in the Pal.

"What about the died garlic in the cooking buckets?" I quizzed Qleo. "Merely endpoints to the vampire's beguine," said Qleo. (We were trading fours.) "Break that off again for me, Qleo, *in modum lascivum*." "You mean, sink some tattle . . ." "Sesame, Nageeb," I said, "into the Boo-Jet Theresa."

"I feel like a large-screen tv," she interrupted, anaesthetized with venison, "in a clinker-built dinghy." Descent was inevitable. "Look at me," I said, "I'm James Joyce with these pennies wedged in my eyes," ". . . singing an aria from 'The Caramel Log of the Dialites,'" Qleo said. ". . . *in modum stupidum*," she said. "I've been washed up on these sands at least twice before," I thought to myself. "Let us to the banks of the Pal repair," Qleo said aloudly. "It's one or the other," she said to these pages. "In the darkened patches of its waves I see villages wrapped in animal fat, but no Pinkl," I said. "I never liked Pinkl," she said, "and the past submits to our sedation of it only because we stupidly sing the harmonies of naïve causal succession."

"Here then, a brief tale, hot-headed Nausicaa," Qleo said, suddenly as oblivious to the Pal as a dogfight fronting a Mennonite choir: "A man hit me once. 'That's one way to treat a man,' I said to him. 'Here's another, I collect them,' he said and knelt before me and gave me a hake from his creel." "Memo to Qleo," she said, "Don't eat the hake."

"Our symposium staggers to its close like the junketing congressman on a bender," I said. "And still no vodka," she said. "And nothing left of the men fighting except our saying they did," said Qleo. "A verbal Kilkenny Cats," I said. "And *still* no vodka," she said. "Your mind = a performance sedan idling on an iceberg," Qleo taunted.

"Only an Alcibiades," I addressed the coruscant Pal, "could silence these fragments."

The clan recruits freshening at the cutbank spigot are as so many jar-headed variations on bible college, gristle-brained manrumbles waiting their turn to swear, "Never again with the animals." And another thing—hell is only the seediest elder of them that gather in the corner of the glassed-in porch to hash off about bourbon enemas and capital gains. How do I know this? A voice come out of a gash in the upholstery of my vehicle that even a dead bird stuffed in bafflewise would not baffle, a voice like unto some rough market of sound from a bakelite radio shoved sideways between leg brace parts and the jarred brain of Abraham Lincoln. It said, and I quote: "Where the action is, there you will find a suction very unlike the indifferent 'thwuck' of the refrigerator door closing on its cold, moist treasure. Go home, boy, and tavern quietly your wife's agitation till it cheese up and bubble into yearning, for only that way lay any promise that the closing oval of spikes rising from the divots she makes in the elegant quadrangle of your trespasses will fast meet and become one spike, and you shall fang your sweet fuck upon it like a receipt."

It ain't never too late, junior, to learn to tail loveliness westward, to where the golden apples core themselves on squirt pine and the moon orbs back with jerks behind soft fenders of the accusing sky, heckling the oracles, making little more of the standard enigmas than you or I when we played chicken in stolen Cadillacs or pressed the pulpy surcharge of last winter's promises into a bouillon cube's worth of sham regret and methamphetamines. At the end of the day the Dalai Lama is only one more kind of coconut dessert telling us that our desires must sooner or later yield to the oily surfaces of death, which accounts for the lithe pinochle of things, so stop complaining. Besides there's always a little bit of untame buried in the audit that the big name help don't know about. You just gotta comb your legs out straight over a chaise lounge and enjoy without misgivings them penultimate gins and tonics, which do to soft lobed evenings pressing lazily against the teak decks of yachts at dusk what a thong does to a pair of uncurdled buttocks. Now be a good haircut and open me a beer, and forget I ever said any of this.

If a boy, in order to decelerate the passage of time, should throw his bicycle into the pond and choose instead to walk under his own power whither he would, a crowd shall suddenly gather and as suddenly proclaim him their long lost philosopher prince. The crowd in exaltation shall then make arrangements for a powerful derrick to lower their own cars into this pond. Soon a mound of cars will be seen to rise from the middle of it, making of the displaced water a navigable moat. "We will once again move along the ground only as swiftly as did our distant ancestors, who dwelled together in a well-constructed citadel surrounded by water," one in the crowd will declaim as if to christen their effort. But if the boy should then ask, "How are you, who cannot swim, going to cross this moat of yours?" the crowd, once again taken unawares and captivated by the new irresistible logic, shall thereupon deliberate in counsel as to who among them should submit to an honorable *noyade*, that, such as choose, their corpses might raise the causeway to their new collective home. A riot shall then ensue, accusations of cowardice and uncivil motives the crowd shall hurl intestine, and a general slaughter commence, which will end only after all are killed but for a single man who, spying the boy under a nearby tree forming letters from blades of grass, shall go to him bellowing: "Look what you've done, you evil boy! Surely these dead, all these dead, surely they will enjoy none of the benefits that accrue to a deceleration of time! Your philosophy is an absolute pestilence. You must be the devil himself!" The boy shall look up and smile an inassimilable smile. "Look here," he will say, "at the number of grass blades it takes to spell my name— exactly twice the number of letters. Therefore, sir, I cannot possibly be the devil." "Right you are," the man, disarmed, shall aver, "My sincerest apologies," and he shall return to the pond and begin the arduous work of building a causeway with the corpses, generally strewn about the place in all the most pitiful postures of unconsidered and arbitrary carnage. That afternoon and evening and well into the night he will labor, remarking to himself more than once, "The boy was right. The boy was most definitely right. It should take exactly this much time, exactly this much, for the new man to reach his true, authentic home."

ALLEGORICAL PORTRAIT OF THE FATE OF AN IMMIGRANT
TO THESE STATES IN THE FORM OF A VENN MEDITATION

Let us describe a set—for our purposes, Set A—as the set of all members who wish
no longer to belong to their native set.

Let us situate Set A suchwise as to grant it a glimpse of the Universal Set, and
construe the occasion such that it is, for instance, a retirement party for said
Universal Set.

Let us next put Set A to blinking rapidly and with unusual force at first glimpse
of the Universal Set. Let this constant and vigorous blinking of Set A, in its
transports at first glimpse of the Universal Set, begin to consume a portion of
its own face while we posit another set—hereafter, simply, Another Set.

Say that Another Set sidles over to our Set A.

Let Another Set be nursing its insouciance in the form of vodka gimlets and vicious
observations as it sidles among the other sets—among them, our Set A.

Let Another Set, along its desultory circuit, address Set A with such words as, "And
you must be the set I've heard so much about . . ."

Allow Set A a more than adequate pause before responding, and then only
stumblingly, "I, um, well, I just . . ."

Let Another Set continue, as if Set A had said nothing: ". . . such that, confronted
with the sight of the Universal Set, your eyes begin to blink away your face
with the ravenousness of a peasant until your constituent members spill out
of your head and go in search of a setless life."

At these words, let the members of Set A begin to flow profusely from its widening
orbits like ants from their domestic mound crushed under heel.

Have it that, with this precipitous exodus of constituents, Set A very soon reduces
itself to little more than a baggy, palpebral flutter, such that Set A is hardly
able to stand for lack of substance.

Have it then that Another Set pretends not to notice the twin cataracts issuing forth from Set A's head but rather feigns a sudden notice of Sets B and M, pardons itself and hurries away in the direction of the bar to freshen its gimlet, redirect its circuit, put its needle to a fresh inflation of innocence.

Let a Prophetic Set, from behind an imposing fence, gaze upon these proceedings with the look of one over-prepared by the gravest of forethought to condemn any and all innovation.

Let the Prophetic Set clutch at the fence, intoning, "This is intersection, this is infamy!" as it watches myriad exiting members of the emptying set A (as for most of whom, let them exhibit a more adroit sense of fashion than their lineage would predict) quickly scatter to ply at mingling and ingratiating.

Have it that several among the guests, amid a spirited quarrel over the composition of the ür-daiquiri, raise a middling digit to the shrill expostulations of the Prophetic Set.

Allow for temporary cantles, brief eddyings, enclaves of setless members thereabouts before the general dispersion, while old Set A flaps alone in the summer breeze like the flag of a forgotten nation.

Let Set A in the course of the afternoon settle eventually over the club grounds and become as a carpet for the other guests.

"What a lovely carpet," let yet another of the sets remark to one of the recently liberated members of Set A.

"I've seen better," have the member say, watching in embarrassment as both his own fellows and other unchary sets trip at the worn edge of a discarded fate now become a carpet, or as is inevitable, merely the destination of fugitive dollops of pâté that would not board the knife toward their appointed cracker.

Between two species of pleasure the connoisseur of pleasures discovers a layer of ash. He tastes the ash. Thinking it another kind of pleasure, he eats of the ash. His powers of intellect capture the feeling of his saliva as it meets the ash and is seduced by it. He chokes on the ash and flails about, upsetting his candle and table in a spastic search for water. He writhes on the floor choking as his house and he are consumed by fire and reduced, in the minds of his friends who come to pick through his charred effects, to a smoldering memory between his search for new pleasures and his recent demise.

But since the search for pleasures is pleasure itself, and personal demise the vestibule to deepest pleasure, two species of pleasure will once again be separated— as any two things: opposites, complements, twins, enemies, times—by a silent, impassive layer of ash.

This is infamy, this is intersection—

At late hours would reconnoiter the Sickness with the Health, as the Sickness was wearing the livery of the Health and the Health that of the Sickness, which they then commenced to exchange for their usual business, though they could not help but let escape many sighs of regrets, the two of them, however laughing enough for their adventures, for there was the Health who never could let off with taking its radiance—poorly concealed in the weeds of sickness—among grave ministers of state for a jolly terror, but came away from the masque wanting a little more effect that only the very Sickness itself could solicit. These ministers saw nothing but liveries, you see, and after such delicious preludes as their alarums and harried briefings, they would dispatch the guileful disguised Health and huddle together in close conference like a bloom shut onto the night, and to the Health's mind the sport of it all was brought too swiftly to an end, and likewise the Sickness, whose miserable ooze but drippingly contained in the clothes of Health, was welcomed in the vestibules and toasted and soon forgotten in all the revelry and drunkenness of them for whom the threat of pestilence echoed but dimly from the forgotten dice cup of sinister agues. So it went for these two compeers, addicted to their constant transvestment, who had so succumbed to the other's charms that all the while it escaped their notice the lining of Sickness had become stained with the radiance of Health, and the garment of Health with suppurative patches of sickness soiled, and it happened in time they met and no longer could ascertain between them whose clothes were whose.

Think about it this whole world slash overlay of too many fates mixed up in a motor voter emulsion it must have everything to do with my inflammation was I talking to you kids try too hard to stuff as much experience as you can into conformity with some appliance ideal might make a Cayman Islands out of the trouble you're in lady but anyway last time I checked survival was more than a scenic overlook so my inflammation right and then I'll stop what is it telling me I've got several what lifetimes are they calling them now to do as they tell me and nail my so-called hands to my head in despair of the "secret disparities of knowledge that gall our way" or sometimes but sometimes not is that it oh balls as if I've never smelled peacock brains on the wind what am I some kind of wrecked vegetable cart of memories you want to steal a tomato huh that wasn't a question

Only when it was nearly extinguished did my sister and I decide we would try to keep a small fire in the sand pit burning as long as we could by pretending we were resuscitating a dying animal. We ran around gathering handfuls of pine needles and sprinkled them gently on the two or three remaining embers of the fire. The needles would flame quickly but were as soon spent. I brought back an old flannel shirt from under my uncle's overturned skiff. My sister took it from me and told me to keep looking for burnable things. "This is our dog," she said, "we can't let it die." "Since when is a fire a dog?" I asked her. "Only this one time," she said to me, "so keep looking for things to burn." I ran away and gathered up some dead leaves and brought them back. "These are good," she said while she looked at them one by one, arranging them in her hands as if they were playing cards. "Go get more." I was looking at the way she had torn the shirt into strips and fed them, along with some lengths of rope and a drinking straw, into one side of the fire. The way these unrelated items led my eye away from the fire had the effect of convincing me I had forgotten which things were combustible and which weren't. "The ends of things are burnable mostly," she said when I asked her what to look for. I felt quite tired all of a sudden and didn't feel in the least like running off in search of the ends of things. "What do you think is burning, the dog or everything else?" she asked me after several minutes. I told her I couldn't tell. "Neither can I," she said, "that's why I think this fire can be our dog." All those places where the tips of the flames disappeared into the air made it difficult for me to hear what she was saying. Her voice sounded like a branch ending in many fine twigs that she was running into the side of the fire along with all the other slender pieces of things she had gathered that went thin at the end. "What goes into this dog's mouth doesn't come out," she was saying, as if she had just discovered her own skin for the first time. "If we say it's a dog, then it must be our dog, and only we can feed it." "I'm finished feeding the dog," I told her, "I'm going inside." "That will only make it more hungry," she said as I was walking toward the house. "Besides, what makes you think you're outside?"

The near remains dark and open to our fury, and sad bowls surround the near. As to the far, we break it blindly and bring it near, and it too darkens. We place it in bowls, the broken far. We light fires and cook down the distance. Warming bowls full of far: these they call our eyes—they who, with eyes on their body, call anything that sees an eye, and look for the body that it's on.

We too once possessed such fashion of eyes, and could gather up the bundled far in them and put a scrutiny to it, each one of us, and belie the tribulation of bringing near the far, and make judgments, each to his own.

However it was, in that time, one of us—our Lycurgus if it please them—had such soil in him as to grow his distanceless interior scrutiny to a size his head could no longer contain, and his eyes were forcibly expelled, became like stemless tubers— otiose, burdensome, gorging themselves on the empty intrigues of culs-de-sac and terminal empires.

Larger and denser his uneyed seeing grew, and there swelled in him a temptation to sheer off the pendulous eyes, and when he did it, very suddenly the nearness of himself brought him comfort, and it was dark and without horizon and full of fury. It was near and everything touched him, and everything touched everything else.

There was not for him but he must then tell—and without eyes on his body—since the near dark could not but tell—a great radish of telling within him, an everything that told, which is all an everything does, there being nothing else left.

And soon the everything hollows, and becomes a bowl, and there is need of a new near—darker than before, darker and nearer, keeping the proximities, the full against the hollow, and the bowls full of far, and a cooking of it with our fury, which must suffice for us who are without eyes, but who must, nonetheless, see.

II

(an epideictic tirade for two voices with extended peroration)

"Man is the animal that talks, but the Cosmos is an Act, not a word."
—Edward Dahlberg

That you hold upside down the book in which these words appear and only pretend to read it merely to avoid the attention of someone whom you dislike represents an indignity to which I shall momentarily respond by means of a set of movements which I generally refer to as a "seizure." You needn't worry, however, that I might cause injury either to myself, or to you, the so called "reader," for that matter: my body knows that it must perform these movements at a certain safe distance both from others and from even the least likelihood that they will do serious harm to me, since the seizure itself, believe it or not, knows exactly how close it may come to causing real injury; and because this is the one and only activity in which I participate that may legitimately lay claim to such knowledge, I feel it necessary to *allow* the seizures to take place, as a matter of precautionary prophylaxis, in the event that I should one day venture close upon a less forgiving and more sudden harm. In fact, to be perfectly forthcoming, it will very likely require more time to explain to you what is about to happen to me vis-à-vis the seizure than the seizure itself could possibly spend happening to me, and then I will no doubt spend an additional period of time explaining this discrepancy to myself and to you, the putative "reader" of these pages, and this explanation should by my reckoning last longer than the previous one, during the course of which a distinct smell of urine will begin to waft from your recollection of previous encounters with me. "How did this odor get in here?" you'll yell inwardly to some of the neighboring recollections, those that hadn't their wits about them sufficiently to merge quickly into an unspecifiable mist of anxiety or nostalgia. "Who went and urinated on this memory?" you'll demand of these standabouts, while I continue on with my sub-seizure of increasingly tenuous explanations, all of it prior to the actual seizure itself. "I am so sick of this!" you'll announce in thought-form to those memories nearest the odor, but they're sick of you too, believe me, and consider these thought-balloon tirades of yours the equivalent of pissing all over *them*. *Your* anger is what strikes these adjacent memories as the misguided urine stream, but in addition, the steady rise in pressure of your shame and frustration at this incontinence, as it occupies a more and more disproportionate amount of room in your private sphere, will press against *their* own collective bladder. I'll hazard that soon the intolerable fact of their residence in your mind will have also become to them a powerful diuretic. So perhaps they've peed on each other—you shouldn't be so astonished, given the middle passage-like conditions many of them have endured day and night from longer ago than they would like to remember.

"Please," you will say to me, while everything is pissing on everything else in your thought-space and making a mess of your interiority, "don't assume that you must now compare this ever widening series of explanations with regard to your seizure to, say, a nest of lipped beakers, or a set of Russian egg figures, or more familiarly, Chinese boxes, because that will only set off an accompanying series of considerations related less by the nesting model than by an arrangement of adjacency, and the thing that happened to you, which you are in the habit of calling a seizure, will feel as though it's adjacent to things that happen to me, and then it will be impossible not to adduce various other modes of adjacency because of the emergence of this feeling, adjacency of similars and dissimilars among these modes, and this endless train of comparisons between you and me will have the effect of erasing my original happiness at being an individual and separate from you, and soon enough you and I will have become the same seizure-wracked person."

Of course, after hearing you say these things, I'll hardly be in a frame of mind to tell you how many times I've had to remind my own single-parent son, on those Christmases that I'm allowed to see him, that he's *not* a fire truck, that just because he happens to be *playing* with a fire truck doesn't entail that he then must *become* one, because every time I remind him of this he insists that he doesn't "happen" to be playing with the fire truck; rather, he has "decided" to play with the fire truck with the intention of becoming one himself before Christmas is over, and if I try to count the number of times we've gone over this and over this, despite seeing him only every other Christmas, I'll no longer happen to have felt the need to relate to you this odd behavior of his but will have convinced myself that *I wanted to* just so that I could become the sort of person that reveals such things to others, meaning that, on the one hand, a situation may arise where, say, several elves have inexplicably decided to end their lives, and that's that. An official issues an order that the elves be removed from public view and properly interred and orders an inquest into the grisly matter, but then suddenly an aerial view reveals that the piles of dead elves dotting the magical kingdom spell out the word "BLAM!" as if in an early period Lichtenstein.

"Portending exactly what?" you'll ask, and with every right, while fighting off an urge to think that I've already morticed and tenoned your private thoughts into the now forcibly clandestine seizure, driven underground by our mutual diffidence, thereby rendering it our *common property.* "A clamp and a hammer," I will bring out, addressing your unvoiced thoughts as only I can, in an allegorized policy of mollification, "are talking to each other . . . no wait a minute, this makes sense," I'll have to insist, "this has point. The clamp is arguing from a perspective for which the hammer has no sympathy, even though both tools, despite their very different appearances, seek to achieve the same ends, that is, the conclusive affixture of two surfaces, planar or curved. There are other tools lying about, watching them, but disinclined to get involved, just looking on like lounging felines. The hammer, an alpha tool in this parable, brings this observation—viz. the cat-like lassitude of the other tools—to bear on his conversation with the clamp, but the clamp doesn't care to honor the hammer's patronizing contributions and continues talking over it. Language is all the clamp possesses in the way of defenses, if we allow for a clamp's structural proximity to the mouth, which can and often does operate according to to the principles of a clamp. But the hammer, surprisingly, seems not to be at all bothered by the rudeness of its interlocutrix, but, just as if he were carrying on a polite conversation, at turns offers his opinions of what the clamp is saying, and in this air of superiority resembles a United States among members of the World Bank of tools. Not until a nearby nail remarks that, whatever they're doing, the clamp and the hammer are certainly not *conversing*, does the hammer 'acknowledge' his anger at the clamp, but chooses to direct his feelings not toward the clamp, but against the lowly and defenseless nail. Such is the way of tools, which consist of masses of *material*, but, tragically for them, are always pressed into the service of a *purpose* of which their materiality can have no understanding. By extension, the orchestrated death of elves in an enchanted kingdom can be profitably understood as a tool-like episode in the *larger drama* being played out at levels of significance that requires something like higher mathematics to be understood, a branch of mathematics yet to be discovered, an as yet purely speculative mathematics."

This brief parable, with explanatory coda, will inspire you to reciprocate in kind. "I knew a man," you will tell me, "who was forever talking about *putting parentheses around* this and that, because *he was no longer satisfied that the prevailing culture could be trusted to decide what was and wasn't a legitimate object*. He put parentheses around *the way he tipped back in his chair at breakfast*, around *certain habits of behavior to which he and his wife were susceptible*. He put parentheses around *the side of the living room that received the most afternoon light*, and another set around *afternoon light in living rooms across the nation*. Soon he was putting so many parentheses around things in his speech and ideas that, with every announcement of the installation of a fresh brace of parentheses, his wife would cry out anew that this affliction of his, this *'parenthesis cancer,'* as she called it, was obtruding on her own fragile ability to maintain the room necessary for respiration and motility. And it was true; he had adduced so many of his own 'objects' that they had not only established within his personal headspace a veritable *world of their own*, but had begun to accumulate with such ferocity from his own environs outward as to give the impression that some pack rat demiurge was at work 'reappointing' the objective continuum according to his own masturbatory compulsions, tucking the jetsam of private experience into every available square inch of unoccupied space; for *private worlds* are indeed both masturbatory and tumor-like in that, even provided the bare minimum of nurture, they will proliferate with such erotic avidity as to crowd the 'you' you had originally thought was you right out of the picture of what you and everyone else had previously considered the objective continuum. Over-attendance to *private worlds* has the effect of exiling one, not just from the polity of the self, but from the entire peninsula of common humanity, so that your average *private worlder*, what with all of the clutter accumulating in his vicinity, will have no choice but to take on the mantle of the prophet and bellow, when he might better whisper, and lard his speech with annoying archaisms, the better, so he autistically assumes, to command the attention of those who have not as yet been granted citizenship in his little dresser drawer of a *private world*. The more enthusiastic one becomes with respect to his *private world*, the more complete his exile from this one, and the less any ordinary citizen will want to keep even the briefest company with him, even though he of the *private world* will always feel called to proclaim the priority of his utterly solipsistic perceptions and judgments, preying on that momentary misjudgment of anyone who makes the mistake of listening to him for even a fraction of a second, becoming the 'Mel who is to be avoided at all costs,' the 'Mel of the unstanched word stream,' that 'Melvin,' or 'Mel' to whom it would never occur to limit to a time frame appropriate for the occasion the great quantity of what he is, at any time of day or night, saying to no one in particular, nor caring in the least whether it might be better to direct his completely obtuse, self-absorbed verbal fusillades to those more inclined to entertain an interest in them than is usually the case. For this 'Mel' sets little store by the protocols of deportment established by age old and statistical usage, which are as little available for even reasoned modification as the pronunciations of words themselves, meaning that this 'Mel's' hapless interlocutors are unable to understand his transgression of these protocols as anything other than gross, prodigious, self-centered violations of time-tested norms."

"—an understanding of the 'Mel,'" I should break in to observe, "that suggests that you have already asked yourself whether your 'Mel'-inspired displeasure might be understood as *your* limitation, and not the 'Mel's'; that this 'Mel' himself might be more aware of the alienating effects of his unobstructed logorrhea than you of your own isolation within the palace of decorum; that he might be in this matter of volubility perfectly transparent to himself and amenable to thinking of his discursive transgressions in say, pentacostal terms, that is, as a heaven sent stream not of wisdom so much as of an unstanched verbiage meant to be taken as an example of what will suffice—like a potassium-based salt substitute—to occupy a mind that would otherwise resort to the violence of tacit unexpressed opinion exerted upon one from impersonal sources."

"Point taken," you will assuredly reply, "and if someone were to approach you in a bookstore and ask, without the least particle of compunction, whether you would, with his announcement that he had shat an eel—better, two eels, a Dioscuri, a Chang and Eng, of eels—take him for having actually shat the eels or for merely mistaking those *fuscous and swimming tubulatures* (words of the 'Mel') for shat eels on account of a complimentarily swimming, i.e. hung over, ken (through which swimmingly refractive glass, shit comes to resemble a Gemini, a Gracchi, a Leopold and Loeb, a Venables and Thompson of eels), and then grant you not even a second to respond before launching into a rhetorical investigation into 'exactly which intelligence might be awakened when, upon looking in a mirror, one (presumably this 'Mel' himself) notices that gills have begun to open along the lower portions of his cheek?'—approached thus, I actively wonder to what degree you would take up the burden to 'know thyself,' and the more so when our 'Mel' continues to ponder aloud 'how one might possibly harness this sudden and spontaneous manufacture of gas-exchanging organs, short of bringing offense to the mouth and lungs? For terrific and, to be sure, unprecedented,' the 'Mel' will continue, 'the pain that ensues at first appearance of superfluous respiratory channels breaking forth among the horse latitudes of the face. And if to give trial to these nascent clefts and dive headlong off a bridge be all the theme of one's initial enthusiasms,' the 'Mel' will speculate, 'what then when, even before turning away from the reflection, spiracles begin to pit the margins of the brow and hairline and a generous array of delicate tubercles commence abristling in star formation from the gentles of the nape outward to shoulders, skull, and spine? What dimension of berth to give,' the 'Mel' will muse aloud, 'to a quick riddling of the extremities with as yet unexploited scuppers giving on to vein and capillary alike; exactly what vintage of live-giving inhalation decanted over these vast branchial grilles newly arrayed across the thoracic veldt, etc.,' with the sorrowful and aggravating effect that the 'Mel's' words will have begun to talk away the material world itself; nothing at all will be safe from the consuming effects of the 'Mel's' words save the 'Mel's' words, and this is exactly what the 'Mel' wants: to reduce the plenary All to his slender, forever evanescent, yet never dying *flatu vocis*; to force us into a situation where, unless we grab hold of this utterly 'Mel'-centered nominalism as onto a weed growing out of a cliffside, we're left to drift for all of time through the 'Mel'-created void, for he will have talked the common world away into a nearly perfect inanity, to a state just shy of complete emptiness, to a dry wind, an idiot mistral of vocables; he will have reduced me to a mere ribbon of shallow breathing, a fragile *Magna Graecia* of minute pressure gradients imperiled by fierce inland tribes; he will have made of me a craven pneumaticide, an edge along an encroaching vacuity, an ineffectual breathing, a meaningless respiration."

How could I help but offer succor by relating to you various failed strategies of my own for avoiding just such 'Mel'-induced mental predicaments, among them my famously ineffective flashcard strategy, for in truth it had sometime ago been a practice of mine to carry on my person at all times many varieties of flashcards—Latin vocabulary flashcards, general anatomy flashcards: in sum, divers flashcards—not in an effort to master any one of these various disciplines—all of which, I must own, bored me to near death—but in a pathetically quixotic effort to lure my thoughts away from topics I would rather not have to consider. I persisted in this strategy, in keeping flashcards on my person at all times and reviewing them diligently at the first sign of mental siege engines gathering near about, with full knowledge that the number of these sorts of diversions ran far short of the vast quantity of topics about which I had decided it would be best to avoid thinking. That my talent for averting my mind from these miasmas was outstripped by the compulsion to entertain them, however, meant that sooner or later I would arrive at the baleful necessity of addressing the unpleasant thoughts directly, and this eventuality was further supported by my avidity at running up the tally of thoughts to avoid at a far faster rate than my ability to find even momentarily effective diversions in the form of fresh sets of flash cards. For one must keep in mind that to him for whom the effort to divert his thoughts could rise to this degree of systematic application, scarce indeed were any theme with which to conduce to such suasion as would necessarily guide him toward an unalloyed delight. Only after dwelling for days in the heat of this admittedly ridiculous impasse did it occur to me that perhaps my chief delight in all this sad world lay in the very effort *to redirect the natural course of my intuitions.*

"Ha, the preposterous lengths we'll go to avoid our own ruin!" I can hear you saying. "Redirect the intuitions? You will as soon redirect the Rhine! Intuitions! What are these little baubles but a mere spindrift floating atop the lifelong, oceanic storm of language, the scheming centerlessness, unopposable, and seditious *industry of words.* They're in league with each other, words; I am certain they conspire to hide each other's mistakes; I swear it, they set up decoys in those tropes and figures of theirs to draw one's attention away from their criminal activity; either they're nothing more than hotel menials stealing silverware and bath towels, or else we've thrown our entire metaphysical fortune to a bunch of Tom Noddy incompetents, allowed to go merrily on their way, unchecked by regulation, unimpeded by suspicion, unwilling to observe even the veneer of etiquette one would have expected from the most predacious Greek, leaving whole ages of disaster in the wake of their so called 'meaning.' Whose house do I dwell in? Who bears the title of my existence? It's as though I entered this life one quiet morning at the bottom of a serene, unmoving pool, the beneficiary of vast research programs devoted to the salutary effects of hydraulic birth, only to have, seconds after parturition, some besotted idiot at the surface commence bombarding me with masses of Bedouin equipage, thinking to offer guidance, to enfeoff my tender youth with a freely held legacy of names and concepts and wisdoms, presuming to rescue me from one vassalage by throwing me into the chains of another. From the servitude of natal barbarism to the forced labor of acculturation. If we had any say in the matter, who would shrink from demanding an immediate return, if not to the foreclosed womb, then to the tit and swaddling clothes, to the dry dug and a torn rag? And what paltry corrective forthcoming from the perennial wisdom? Deeds rather than words, the perennial wisdom adjures. Words, the debased ersatz deed; deed, the fulfillment, the destiny of words. So much for common wisdom, whose perenniality, it seems, has left it exposed to addlement and worms. For only words remain after the mayfly life of the deed expires. In a spasm of unintended heroism, the soldier takes the hill, and for the next forty years Mr. Cincinnatus tinkering in his car port retakes the hill *ad infinitum*, courtesy of the pliant, ever ingratiating word, scheming away in its ant farm memory, until the hill is eroded into a depression and Mr. Cincinnatus hangs himself in the attic for want of another hill to take. A scummy residuum, a creepily disciplined band of opportunistic hangers on, words—or so the muscle-bound, jar-headed deed would have one think. And please, no more about *speech centers* in the brain, no more about the linguistic *hard-wiring* of the brain. If the real-estate Satan gazes down upon a lush, unspoiled river valley and pronounces it *hard-wired* for waterfront development, if the meat packer, watching as an unresisting herd debouches without rebellion straight into its own demise, pronounces the hoofed genera *hard-wired* for slaughter, one will hardly expect the word-drunk neuroscientist, after drawing a pint of gibberish from the forebrain of some unfortunate with a tap of electric current, to deduce that the human is hard-wired rather to burrow into the earth and prepare for death, though he would with that conclusion have come closer to the truth. There exists no single intelligible word, just as there exists no single knowable self, and congeries of words, like congeries of selves, are productive of nothing so much as mass delusion. The vicious *deus absconditus* vested us with this grenade-lined smoking jacket of linguistic prerogatives and then traipsed off behind the kitchen door to watch all of the explosive fun and, more importantly, to shield itself from all the logic-chopping gore. The explosion of silence into this rodential pullulation of meanings—infantile creation myths, idiot formularies, one-size-fits all Neo-Platonisms, tiresome phenomenologies, ludicrous poetries, arrogant sciences—a flood tide of assertions: no wonder the kabbalist's *Ein-Soph*, divine and absolute perfection, god of God, turned tail toward sanctuaries inaccessible to mind, purely out of embarrassment for having given rise to this deafening palaver, thick with its own futility. No wonder the increate *One* of Plotinus, from which flows the travesty of the many, resists direct contemplation: scandalized by the stupidities emanating from what it had presumed was its perfect innocence, it set up a fulgurating glory to distract the worshipful masses while it was off scouring the empyrean in frantic search for a tourniquet strong enough to tie off the offending flow. Being is a wound agush from an artery in the thigh of the divine, who is a wound in the thigh of primordial silence, which was the first and only instance of etiquette in this beastly cosmological epoch. The old-time sky god positively refreshes. Give me an unequivocating Zeus, give me the angry Jehovah, the furious Ahura Mazda, a volley of thunderbolts, the percussion of natural cataclysm. Give me the Hundred-handed, squeezing fistfuls of men at a time into arable humus. Give me the testicular rain of Ouranos, a furious hosing down of the worldwide verbal conflagration . . . Fruitless! The verbal conflagration only clears the way for a tilling of ground, for a spreading of seed, a tending of shoots, and a harvesting of yet more bread to feed the verbal conflagration. The source of these insights must lie somewhere in my legs, for it most often occurs while walking that I will be brought to a sudden halt by the enormities visited on conscious existence. These enormities, these villanies of the natural order, though they outstrip the mind by their size and sheer pervasiveness, are to the legs perspicuous enough to bring them to a staggering and complete halt. Even *my* legs, unheavily cabled as they are, little more than poorly bundled twigs, during the warmer months the object of persistent ridicule among women, even these eczematous hobbling stilts—with what sensitivities they are endowed! I would not be the least surprised if it were in some tendon of the ankle that the thinking substance were located, if it were discovered that, lo these many years, an ankle tendon had, out of modesty and patriotic devotion, been funneling intelligence to the cortical zeppelin, that an unassuming tendon deep within the ankle or wrist had proved Athenian to the Mede of invading sense data. Often, as I say, these closet ministers, my legs, will draw me to a sudden, stupefied halt, seized by the realization that, in the end, I have no idea who or what I am. 'In the end—' what could that possibly mean? What end? There is no end. There is no such end, and yet the lemming slash bondservant slash under-educated musculature of the mouth finds these meaningless tags irresistible. The drudge *buccinator*, the peon *depressor anguli oris*, the lackey *depressor labii inferioris*, the mule *levator menti*, the subaltern *zygomaticus minor* and *major*, the menials *levator labii superioris* and *alae nasi*, the retarded cabin boy *risorius*, and of course, the most disgustingly slavish hack of them all, the stooge *tongue*—all these mindless custodians and stewards of the speech act, extending and contracting in the most intricate concert, these idiot-savant tensors and extensors that carve their Cellini saltcellars out of a puff of air without having the least notion of what they're doing! What a travesty of cooperative effort! Such a baroque articulation of brute, meaningless effort—into equally meaningless meanings! Only under duress, under the sign of despotry, such a well-regulated *corvée*! Every phoneme is driven to its sentence by blows! Only a pharaoh could harness such a motley of disparate, mulish wills. The Pyramids, the Great Hall at Karnak? Of clay and wattles made, beside the lexical Panopticon. Wittfogel's thesis is best applied to human physiology: the drooling of pre-reflective man threatened him with a fatal dehydration until the advent of speech; therewith the birth of measurement, the invention of the sluice-gate: speech as nothing so much as a sophisticated curb for the Nile of drool and fetid breath upwelling from the face of man. As I say, my legs will bring me to a full stop momentarily along the boulevards—the word *boulevard*, oh yes, what a beautiful word: one thinks of mature sycamores in rows, of brick sidewalks, of young couples walking hand in hand, of horse-drawn carriages for the tourists, several lanes of traffic: *boulevard*, a primary concept for the peaceable city. But beware, my friend, recall the friendly industrial arts teacher, to whom all the students turn for advice, not knowing him for the convicted rapist that he is. Very like, this word *boulevard*, properly a walkway along the top of a rampart, a street occupying the site of demolished fortifications. Current meanings are foodstuffs broken down into a feces by forces beyond anyone's power to manipulate. No, strike that—current meanings are the visible portion of an immense convection pattern of solid waste from a meal consumed and digested long ago during some antediluvian, pre-semantic golden age: *bulwark* one minute, *boulevard* the next: we're worse off than the infant who plays in his own caca: we wallow in somebody else's: we build our little paradise on the shifting feces of a Moorlock's acre. I can find no firm ground. Fleetingly, I will stop and have the most pleasant experience of having found my footing, but a moment later to my horror, the realization will be borne in upon me that I have either trespassed on someone else's footing or given birth to yet another wind egg of spotty thinking. This isn't a question of petty ownership. If it were to turn out that I had been borrowing someone else's footing all this time, fine. What do I require aside from food, shelter, and some little surety against making a complete ass of myself by claiming that I've found my footing. One footing per person, we're told as children—individuality and all that. How many footings, authentic, individual footings can one find in recorded history anyway? Orpheus? Borrowed (dreamy songstruck adolescent). Socrates?

Borrowed (obsessive inquisitive toddler). Alexander? Borrowed (overweening pageant queen). Jesus? Borrowed (underweening etiolated nursemaid). Julius Caesar? Borrowed (overweening adolescent opportunist). Genghis Khan? Borrowed (steroidal hirsute Alexander). Napoleon? Borrowed (steroidal homuncular Genghis Khan). Beethoven? Borrowed (songstruck steroidal overweening post-adolescent). Einstein? Borrowed (hirsute dreamy steroidal Socrates). All these specious footings must have descended from a single, immense error . . . the word *immense*, I've been using the word *immense* for years now, use it quite often, in fact ('in fact—' You see, I simply cannot stop preening!) things often strike me as *immense*, except for those things I wish were actually *immense* ('actually—' Have I no shame?) How about an immense pleasure every now and again, how about one immense pleasure? Of course, never in all the time I had used the word immense, not until this very moment, did I notice that it was only one more negative concept, just another crumb, another shaving fallen from my incessant gnawing away at the indifferent *Nought* (or *Gnawt*, as the orthographical crow flies). *Immense*: not admitting of measurement. Now I consider it beyond dispute that the vanishingly small is every bit as immeasurable as the immeasurably large, and that the immensely large may lay a claim to an infinity every bit as boundless as the dimensionless minimum. Yet for the immeasurably large we reserve the word *immense*, while for the immeasurably tiny we prefer *infinitesimal*. Since when does an infinity stretch only in the direction of diminishment? Our moronic habits of usage would answer, 'only since immeasurability decided it would mingle exclusively with gargantua.' Oh, but these asymmetries are positively vomitous to me. Then again, it would appear I'm not above taking a taste of my own vomit—an evolutionary vestige of the quadruped, no doubt. I'll have another lick or two of what I've failed to digest, I'll have another go at my auto-Phlegethon of hork-chowder, but it terrifies me, this shitty pseudo-knowledge, this scow of verbiage, in which I am daily compelled to place my good faith and trust. Oh, that I could exhume the fresh remains of that primordial and anonymous proto-'scholar' who must have made up his mind that . . . yes, exactly:

made up his mind, *the* mind, the pluming arrogant *sfumato* of mind; if only we could disinter this palaeolithic Spinoza, scatter the limbs and midsection of this father of casuistry who would presume simply to make up, for a squeamishness in the face of vivisection—theater of the one truth—this vast verbal substitution, just adduce it out of thin air—rather expelled, violated, phonated air. All hail Vesalius, who couldn't wait for the noble's death rattle before setting to, blade in hand, with a spirited autopsy. All hail Vesalius, and a battery of curses on Thoth, protector of scribes, that phratry of sedentary poltroons. Thoth, fittingly the baboon god—that is, when he isn't busy being the ibis god and giving himself an enema with his own beak. Only mitochondrial Eve could have wrought worse havoc. After all, who knew what might come of some innocent cytoplasm and a few organelles? A particle of concentrated mischief in the unmolested earth. Who could have known? Likewise, the innocuous adverb, the least piddling conjunction, a mere vowel gradation, they all whittle away at whatever punkwood substance I might momently posit as my own, they water my wine, they clip the coin of my realm. My travails serve as nothing more than an intermezzo for the grammatical Versailles. My anguish, disfigured for life by the thalidomide of verbal sublimation, is mistaken by the court of words for a physical comedy. The forced march from subject to predicate provides the only passage into an acknowledgement of existence, while simultaneously bastardizing it beyond recognition. Often I will stop for a moment after a long walk along the bowdlerized thoroughfares, stunned that I have successfully disproved that I am me. I could have as easily proved that I was you, which would amount to the same thing—an equipollence of creditable proof and disastrous nonsense, both composed of faulty elements shot through with fissures and methane. We plume ourselves by dismissing the chapters on phrenology in Hegel's *Phänomenologie* . . . not stopping to contemplate that the subject-predicate farce will to the minds of an otherwise lamentable future appear as silly as phrenology does to us, who were not so long ago mesmerized by the craniometries of the racist, by aethers and phlogistons and leechings. *Phrenology* and *Phenomenology*: from a distance they resemble each other sufficiently to be mistaken for the same word, which should hardly offend. To equate a naïve science of appearances with the baseless cartography of skulls I count as no greater intellectual miscarriage than to have theorized shamelessly about the *unqualified freedom of self-consciousness*—and by means of endless unintelligible qualifications, no less! By slenderest contingencies to the Absolute! By séance to the land of the dead! By thimble boat to the realm of faeries! By words to the Kingdom of Nothing but More Words, *in the end*, which is no end, which is nothing but the grossly elongated colon of the word collective. The word collective devours us and shits us out of its infinitely extended posterior. The arduous mental journey by dialectic merely recapitulates a squeezing of the little bit of life allotted to us through the light years–long rectum of the word collective. The groans of the constipated word collective forcing us through its unending anus drone on interminably like the conclusion of a symphony that ends and ends and ends with no end. Where was I? Oh yes, one needn't hire out an Aquinas to dispatch with irrefutable finality the substance of the self as little more than a bovine faith in the concept of self, which everyone, including me, has acquired by dint of using the word *self* without cease. The gas bag Windham said, in a moment of inadvertent lucidity, 'There is nothing so true as habit.' I would only add that, after having been groped and leered at by the nard-heavy seraglio of philosophical concepts, all the Ganymedes and stable boys in royal livery that haven't any relation to truth whatsoever, not even an antithetical one, these blind or drunk or accidental collisions with truth on the part of habit constitute an intimacy unto unity. Where was I? Oh yes, the exploration of selfhood always has about it the atmosphere of that ominous period just prior to the passage of legislation authorizing the institution of government-issued identity cards. There always hangs about investigations into the structure of the self a sense that the dissolution of an *ancien régime* approaches, that old liberties will soon be revoked, a Weimar of fertile ignorance overthrown, and a program of national identity cards established. Attempts to survey the perimeters of selfhood, expeditions to gather from the supposed depths of personality samples of the slimy bathybius that lubricates the unconscious drive shaft, are almost always accompanied by peculiar anxieties, an elongation of shadows, ominous footsteps, intimations of corridors, autumns and barren wombs, and a fascistic issuance of identity cards. The more consideration one gives to the matter, the clearer it becomes that to plumb the lower reaches of selfhood is merely to determine the thickness of a government-issued identity card. An ambivalence among the citizenry at the issuance of identity cards signifies both a fear on the part of the citizenry that the self consists of nothing other than possession of said card and a desperate wish to possess the card as the one reliable token of selfhood, so little space need be devoted to proving the equivalence of the two. The word *self* has no more heft to it, has no greater dimensions than a 3" by 2" photo ID card. A self, recognized as such apart from a government issued card with raised stamp, is nothing more than a basilisk of psychological unity, with fatal halitosis intact. The self of the modern, entertainment-fed, post-industrial state will escape from a cyclopean cave of unconscious automatism only on the wooly underbellies of identity cards issuing like sheep from the government presses. But let us not stray from the interval of disquiet immediately prior to this eventuality, full of febrile debates about infringements on life and property, teeming with lay analyses of entrenched power and disenfranchised faux-Ezekiels whose words, trailing with streamers and unexamined passions, give the appearance of ragged Portuguese men-of-war floating in dire caravans out of their mouths, all this while an archipelago of isolated Volpones retool in anticipation of a swift black market in identity cards, for though the populace will appear to bristle with the indignation one would expect from the myth-dependent, obtuse self, it is all but certain that they will be busy with cormorant enthusiasm securing a ready source of identity cards for them and their loved ones. A complex suffusion of dread and pointless industry, why is this all so familiar . . . of course! The prelude to orgasm. Ah, orgasm, that dusty bibelot, nestled among memories of home milk delivery and leaded gasoline, of boy guiding hoop with stick down poplar-bordered lane into ambush of other rock-throwing boys; orgasm, a flash of ormolu in the flea-market memory, but to the point: those seconds, perhaps minutes immediately prior, when subtle shivers would pass along the length and width of my young body, pleasurable wavefronts of shivers that cut this way and that like veering, cutaneous zephyrs: up from the heel, down from the occiput, straight across the torso, oftentimes following the paths of the more turbid currents of eczema and psoriasis, but often fording these, a mountain thermal rippling at right angles the Rio of Herpes Zoster that effectively divided me into northern and southern regions, the whole body—yes, even my equatorial zone of shingles—vibrating under these myriad vectors of electrical cilia, quivering beneath this filigree of shivers, asking in effect, 'What need for the orgasm itself?' And I noticed betimes, as they whipped hither and thither, that these sensations possessed definable shape, were not so much like winds as closed figures, however variable the angle at which they cut from one side or extremity to the other of me, and as my capacity to discern the path and angle of them intensified, I found that a two-dimensional surface would no longer suffice to map their course and began to trace their careers as if in a three-dimensional volume, for I had discovered that to liken them to clearly defined flocks of birds—*murmurs* of birds they are called, those shape-shifting aerial nets one sees flying from one side to the other of a highway—these murmurs most perfectly captured the character of their movement. My discernment continued to improve, and it was not long before this flocking gave way to the odd revelation that they were in truth shadows of individual birds, or birds themselves of an unprecedented sort. Verily, orgasm was converting me wholesale into an aviary! Wingtip at thigh, beak at lower lip, crest at crotch, this parliament of fowls that cut the airy way, these swallows, crows, finches, the occasional crane (the turbulence of whose flight from one end of me to the other would leave standing waves of a most intense sloshing behind it)—they made straight into my senses five; indeed, I began to taste the oil in their wings, I detected an odor of carrion in the vulture's feathers, I heard the rustle of the junko's pinion at my temples; they were thick upon me, filthy things, the chattering, the tick-infested wings, the closeness of it all! An uncertainty as to whether I contained them or they me ripened into the disgust one should properly feel for birds. The whole nauseating preparatory put me entirely off orgasms. Overcome by an avifaunal claustrophobia, castrated by shivers, it bore in upon me that I should turn again to a cultivation of my eczema, my St. Anthony's Fire, my impetigo, and forswear the orgasm. Surfeit of birds, surfeit of words, one palls as much as the other, and all things trend toward a glut. Give me air! Return me to my *self*. There at least is a vacuum the human nature has yet to teach itself to abhor—how could it, how to picture a maliciousness between vacuums, how delineate a brawl between inanities? I must remind myself: one needn't stand on top of the Matterhorn, one need not contemplate the pulsars and nebulae to get a good look at Pascal's terrible spaces: every sentence we utter is riddled with them, excretory and terrible spaces. Next to the gap between two words, an expedition to Aldebaran and a kindergarten field trip to the firehouse are indistinguishable. The gauche convenience of selfhood reminds one of the pump at the side of the mini-mart advertising 'FREE AIR.' The talking animal is a hawker of wind, after all is said and done. 'After all is said and done—' please, what is said falsifies, and what is done is done in the service of that falsification. What is the larynx but the lowest entrepreneur in a Marrakesh of expediency carrying on its lamentable trade in the meanest stuff imaginable—dirt maybe, or scraps of cloth? What am I but a patsy for laryngeal crimes, felonies of unintended meaning committed in my name? What a hopeless, utterly risible situation: I plead for a justice that only my scourge can dispense! I am hedged 'round by semantic treacheries. Daily I relive the substance of the 'Helot' parable. Only in terms of the 'Helot' parable am I able to fathom indignity upon indignity folded into the vulnerable myocardium. 'Beating leagues of monotone,' the poet wrote, holding a conch to his ear, but he could as well have been speaking for the steady assault upon the heart by wave after wave of misrepresentation and aporia, captured so deftly in the old parable of the 'Helot,' which I quote in full:

Some very young boys were throwing stones at a group of swans. A man walking by, understandably upset at their brutality, yelled at them, "How about I throw stones at you?" "How about you suck my dick?" one of the boys replied, and without the least hesitation. Well, the man was so shocked—as much at the swiftness with which the boy had delivered the riposte as at his insolence—that at first he couldn't speak. There he stood, effectively silenced by these little boys while they went on stoning the swans. He finally collected himself sufficiently to ask them, "Who taught you to say such a thing, how old are you?" "Who taught you to ask so many questions when there's dick to be sucked?" another of the boys answered as promptly as the first had. They all giggled and turned back toward the water. Again, the man was as much astonished as angry, for in his mind the extreme youth of these boys would seem to have guaranteed a certain measure of innocence. "You just cannot speak that way to perfect strangers," he insisted with a tone of voice that suggested he would have stamped his feet, if he weren't obliged to project an image of authority. Their collective indifference to these admonitions, however, struck him as a physical impossibility, as though it were in violation of some incontrovertible law. "Suppose you tell us just what to say then, dime-fuck," a third boy said, at this point not even suffering to turn around toward the man. It was clear that with this last remark they intended to be finished with him, for they began to shower the swans with handfuls of stone, laughing the while and talking to each other. The man hadn't noticed it before, but the swans seemed actually to encourage the pelting, for they would swim in the direction of whichever boy had a fistful of stones and crane their necks to meet the fanning projectiles. "Why don't you leave the boys alone?" a woman said from inside a car parked nearby. The man turned around quickly. "They're throwing stones at the swans!" he yelled, holding still to his conviction that, aside from any complicity on the part of the swans themselves, such activity was uncivilized, and certainly not the thing to foster in boys. The woman's face told clearly how ridiculous she thought he was. "They're stoning swans. They like it. They're raised to like it." "That would hardly seem to make it right," he tried to paint in muted tones his distaste for the peremptory manner in her response. "Well I suppose that's a matter for you to take up with whoever raised them, but yelling at little boys certainly isn't going to accomplish anything." "So you're not the mother of these boys?" the man persisted, but the woman's attention was suddenly and, so the man thought, a little too deliberately, captured by a detail of prison inmates who had just arrived to rake up the garbage along the shore. They had only disembarked from the van when the boys immediately threw down the pebbles they were holding and ran to the rear of it where rakes and bags were being distributed. "Hey, jail faggots," they began to yell at the inmates from several yards away. Soon they were hurling extraordinary insults and laughing and hanging moon with ferocious insolence. "Wanna skewer a little o' this kay-bob?" one of them taunted. They took up sticks and simulated so brutal and stylized a form of masturbation with them that the sticks were rapidly decorticated and the white inner wood revealed, which seemed to inspire the boys to begin whipping each other in the buttocks. If the man's disgust was at all mitigated by having at first witnessed the swan episode, it only intensified the longer he waited for some sort of reprimand from one of the adults, but the prisoners only laughed quietly and talked among themselves, while the warden, smiling and waving to the woman in the car, threw a single pebble at one of the boys' bared buttocks in playful provocation. The boy turned around and thrust out his mandible momentarily with a terrifying shriek, and then laughed and started after the warden, threatening him with parallel streams of verbal abuse and urine, both many times more forceful than one would have imagined a seven-year-old could produce. The warden jogged playfully backward and eventually came side to side with the woman in her car, who was driving up from behind him approaching a line of poplars among which, as it happened, the man had come to rest, as if exhausted by the effort of containing what he was resigned to accept as his utterly useless remonstrances. "You're one of that sort, aren't you," the woman said to *him with a sneer as she drove up alongside. "You're an individual, all full of interior worlds and courtesy. I suppose you have heroes." "What I don't have is the slightest notion of what you might possibly mean by that," the man spat out. "Even the most depraved pederast would be horrified by those boys." "Those boys," she mimicked witheringly, "will soon be so round and polished that when people look at them, they'll see only their own image. That, little man, is the virtue that comes of mutual attrition, but you wouldn't know about such things. You have your worlds to attend to. But, then again," she said, looking off away from him toward the boys and revving her engine, "into the soft tissues of every individual a little gall wasp must fly," and she threw a handful of stones at his face and drove away in the direction of the prisoners.*

The 'Helot' parable: an unflinching summation. After reading it aloud I could as well cut my tongue out and throw away my pencil for all I care, that would suit me just fine—anything to silence me, anything to forestall the inevitable descent into lyricism. The threat of lyricism hangs over each and every utterance. No matter how rude, fustian, discontinuous, incomprehensible, mean, or uncharitable, the superadded component of song will finally put a stake in the heart of even the least claim to legitimacy on the part of any and all utterance. That every art, as the cliché goes, should aspire to the condition of music says less about the preeminence of music than it does about the crapulousness, the thorough dissipation of the other arts. One can picture them gathered around the piano, arms linked, holding their glasses in the air while they sing about the good old days when a republic of the arts still stood, before the usurpation of consciousness by music, the ubiquity of which only cheapens those occasions when one makes the deliberate choice to listen to it. The refinement of the emotions, the unity and substance of sentiments, the viability of the consciousness, all stand in grave peril with this complete invasion, this taking by siege, this autocracy, on the part of music. What have we wrought? Our cerebrospinal fluid swims with mindless rhythms, our every tear has a ballad suspended in it like a sibyl in an ampoule, the air will soon be little more than a passing tone to the arrogant lung. I have acquaintances who think of the successive stages of life in terms of sonata form, others who see in passing clouds, in arthropodal anatomy, in traffic patterns, the intimations of symphonic structure. You see, not only are the multitudes given over to this lunacy but the scholars too, and the artists. An irrevocable musicalization of experience is rapidly clear cutting all the old growth textures of awareness and, what is worse, laying waste to the positive value of silence, which we know now as nothing more than the absence of music. One can hardly blame the brain-heavy animal for this sad development. It is all with the brain, with keeping its baroque and coffered surfaces filled to the brim, as if these recesses, these gaping, ravenous laquearia, were little more than ice cube trays standing at the ready for a cocktail party that never comes to pass, while the eyes— that shallow, expectant couple with very few thoughts of their own—stand peering out the window, waiting pathetically for the first non-arrivals. Deny the brain one worldly concern, and something else will as soon have filled in the resulting vacancy, and what better as an all-purpose filler than sound, and what better variety of sound than a memorable one, and what more memorable one than music, which will, very soon, have displaced every other variety of comestible in the larder of the mind. All things are forever passing from a state of mewling potentiality to one of obnoxious realization. Allow me to amend that: all things are forever passing from one botched realization to another. All is flux, indeed, to the contemporary mind—more accurately, a reflux, a catarrh played upon a guitar, blue with the multiple contusions visited upon our St. Cecilia by her Corybantic admirers. We have grown so used to ambient song that we are thrown into unease and stupor in its absence. Our very physics has been demoted to a medieval symbolism, a primitive schematic, a caricature, of the musical hypostasis. We will take the infinite primordial density of the fetal universe for little more than the archangel's embouchure, and the subsequent explosion his deafening reveille. The twinkling stars herewith become an etude of infant fingers among wind chimes, the vault of the zodiac passing overhead a caravaneer's ode. The argument is sound that mimics the easy satisfactions of a perfect cadence. We finish our thoughts in thirty-two bars. Perplexity only connotes the odd meter. A young couple dining in silence provides the contemporary allegory of strife. As the greater portion of our daily activities moves within doors and seasonal imperatives grow dim in the memory, our calendars will be supplanted by *rondo* structures designed to tranquilize, and this superimposition shall not cease until our consciousness has become so thoroughly musicalized that the signal to relieve one's bladder will have taken the form of an *appoggiatura*. Dismiss all of this at your peril: understand the plaiting together of disparate global interests as other than a feminization, a lyricization of the war drive, construe the terms and dimensions of experience itself as anything other than the developmental legacy of the well-tempered nerve, but recall the force with which a scrap of tune brings a moment in your own distant past to the forecourt of your attention, irrespective of your own wishes. Music has replaced smell as the royal road to the unwanted and inaccessible past. A demon synaesthesia, music, a panaesthesia that will soon overrun capital and farflung province alike. And as if all of these intrusions by music into activities and matters that have nothing to do with it weren't enough, one has constantly to defend his sanity against incessant retellings of the Orpheus myth, the proliferation of which is difficult to fathom. A remnant of our fabric must be resisting the musical saturation, it must be that we wish to warn ourselves of some imminent loss but possess no other means than to repeat the Orpheus myth over and over until we have collectively become an Orpheus within a larger Orpheus myth. Always on the verge of losing a most precious possession, very likely for thinking it a possession, we play and replay this anxiety in the form of retellings and exegeses of the Orpheus myth. Such is the method and ignorance of our self-involutions: to foregird ourselves against pending loss by an autistic homeopathy of circumstance. So bent are we on conquest and rapine that by a sympathetic assumption of their identity we think to insulate ourselves from the misfortunes of others. Here is the supinity that journeys to hell, Chablis in hand, and returns later that evening to broil the striped bass. Because we cannot or will not understand eventualities as other than a matter of possession or deprivation, because cupidity reigns over all the other predicates of human nature, because wisdom is but another variety of avarice, we couch Macbeths, who have acquired our ill-got, language- and music-sodden- consciousness merely by looking and listening, we shall lose our dominion of awareness as swiftly as we acquired it. Yet some small faction in the constitutive mob of *personae* each of us has devoured knows this; thus are we haunted. Though we cannot think of value in terms other than profit and loss, and therefore cannot clearly define what it is we are afraid we shall lose, other than something we might have gained, we are haunted; thus the haunted condition, which is nothing other than the mythological condition, the pupating condition—wrapped in a cocoon of vague worries striated with presumptions and admonitory tales. A mythologico-musical consciousness that has survived, like the appendix, well into a post-mythological epoch! Perhaps it intuits its own demise, this song-irrigated spirit, perhaps like the wounded beast that finds a covert to spend its final moment, our sensibility is, as I speak, hollowing its death grail out of the Orphic *descensus Averni* without our knowing. The mortally injured wolf circles in the bitter vetch before lying down to die; the human perseverates on the theme of Orpheus. Tightening circles of compulsion and habit: thus the Malebolge we shall soon occupy with the Adam of our most trusted companion. Yet of its impending loss the wolf remains silent, an instinctual Stoicism in stark contrast to the verbose rehearsal for our de-Eurydice-ization, she who shall in a most compensatorily abbreviated and utterly enigmatic moment be plucked from our side, as if all of our experience up to the moment in question had been an anomaly, a fabricated interregnum of half-truths between flanking eternities, as if these sibling eternities had been at work behind a veil they had thrown over our eyes, grinding and polishing the interval between them into a moment of enigmatic perfection, a temporal gemstone faceted with forms of loss, with dematerializations and divestments. *She shall be reft from us, for we have not loved her well enough.* It may be morning, it may be afternoon, it may be evening—an evening, let us say for the sake of argument. Home, office, car—in the car let us situate them; for the immediate purpose it hardly matters. We—the collective Orpheus—and our Eurydice, let us put them in a supermarket parking lot some night on the way home from their diversionary where ever. As is typical of the husband, meaning the congealed us, he will not be torn from the radio, and so as always it shall be Eurydice, only a little irritated, who must to the store alone, that he may remain behind, comfortable in plush interiors, allowing the stray pang of conscience to register between phrases of his musical preoccupation (oh no, our hero does not play, nor compose, but only listens, only grazes), just as minutes later, he will but glancingly notice her departure from the same set of double doors, carrying the grocery bag as always, not cradled in two arms but in one hand, as if it were her lunch. And among these fragments of his awareness, nothing out of the ordinary shall register until she begins to veer in a direction away from the car, without the least indication in her face or movements that she might be entertaining bizarre gestures or weird unannounced plans of escape, but rather as though the global coordinates themselves had shifted, such that our hero was no longer where he had been when she entered the store; though again, in the event of such an absurdity, she would necessarily show some evidence of confusion, would stop walking for a moment and look about, yet she will do nothing of the kind, but proceed in the most unremarkable fashion to the left side of a car her husband will never before have seen and pull from her purse a set of keys. If his attention had been mottled with other involvements up until the moment she arrived at the door of this car, he will now view with unblemished clarity and mounting confusion the removal of keys from her purse, the unlocking of the door, everything, as I say, as if parts of a routine so familiar as to be followed without thought, and at this stage of what he will assume must be some sort of practical joke at his expense (isn't that his way, to presume that what he doesn't understand may be dismissed as an elaborate contrivance), he will get out of their car, smiling no doubt as he makes his way across the immaculate pavement, grinning nervously out of embarrassment that he is about to suffer the indignity of unwanted surprise. Darkness and the glare from the mercury vapor lamps reflected in the windshield will obscure her face as he approaches. This will bother him later, that he could not determine from her expression whether she might be watching him, smirking, or wearing some more ominous expression. Within the time it takes for him to reach the driver's side window, she will have deposited her purse on the passenger seat and inserted the key into the ignition, turning it exactly as her eyes meet his. She will appear quite surprised, wary, as if a stranger were approaching her, and the simultaneous ignition will amplify these alarms. He will knock at the window and signal her manually to bring it down, which, as she does only a little at first, will draw her face closer to his. The combination of her fear and puzzlement will begin to frighten him, and though for a brief moment he may recover some small self-possession with the thought that she must be about to present the car to him as a present (again, could he greet the unanticipated as anything other than a gift?), the lack of significant occasion will quickly erode any force in this hypothesis. There will be no birthday to celebrate, no anniversary to mark, their own car will have been in perfect working order. He will run a string of these frantic suppositions alongside his quick, severe bafflement, and only after she lowers the window a bit more, discreetly locking the doors beforehand (the sudden, simultaneous descent of the four mechanisms will have the effect later, in his recollection, of a portcullis lowering between him and the intimacy he might once have enjoyed with any certitude whatsoever) will she ask him hesitantly, and with a tone of some annoyance, 'Can I help you?' The inflection in these words will bring home to him, shudderingly, that this is no joke, and the blood will begin to drain into his feet. He will shake his head violently and ask 'What's going on?' and say her name with the rise in pitch of an interrogative, and she will squint her eyes and, repeat, 'Can I help you? Do I know you?' She will thrust her face closer toward the window: not a grain of recognition will show. Another woman will have arrived at the rear of a van parked to the left and watch him suspiciously. "What are you doing, whose car is this?" he will demand of her angrily. At this, she will bring the window back up, and look down briefly to shift the car into low gear, again with no hesitation, as if she had driven it for years while cultivating, for the sake of inexplicable illusion, the appearance that she had yet to learn how to operate a manual transmission. She will look up at him once more very briefly; her eyes will have grown a shade darker than usual, not that they will 'flash' or appear as suddenly possessed of devils, but at that moment a suspicion will rise in him, but then sink again as quickly, that those aren't her eyes—anything to explain a substitution, for a moment later she will drive away, and he will never see her again, and he will rage, as I have raged, until he/my citizenship within the empire of conscious awareness has lost all savor, all definition, until my rage has ground me to a fine powder and you and I are by the breeze of a passing car thoroughly commingled, and we with all the others, all the strangers, and we will have returned then to an aboriginal unity. We will no longer drink deeply of horizons and wholes but serve as insensible functionaries, our ears and eyes, all the grandly adorned vestibules and chapels into the great apse of mind fallen to dust, the last vestiges of our uniqueness erased, until we each have arrived at our final undifferentiated vocation, to pour, each one of us, a single microtone into the universal panphony of void, the beginning, the middle, and the end of which shall sound at once and for all time, a monotonous drone of indifferent, anaesthetized spheres. But be not afraid, we will no longer batten on even the echo of fine distinctions, for they will have died away long since, and our seizure will have ended. Those our separate selves, as you foretold, will have been melted into an undying, invariable hum, and like the baseless arguments for our enduring, we shall be dissolved in the wrack of our inheritance, and all our warring charms o'erthrown, and what strength we have shall be most faint."

III

The first movement consisted of an allowance for movement. Even stillness has its siege tactics.

*

I have been raised to think of my fate as a stranger encountered on a train who happens to be reading the same book as I, *this* book in fact, which writes itself by being read on a train by two strangers unaware of something of tremendous importance that must remain hidden for the sake of that importance, the hiddenness of which is exactly *this* importance.

*

Your memory, my memory, their memory—behind the *unchanging* word lies the truth of subjective experience, from which vantage it would appear that *we* are being experienced, that in Lockean terms, *we* are mere secondary qualities, though as to the sensorium to which one can attribute us, that must remain unknown . . . an unknown adventure in the life of the partially known.

*

The self betrays itself so predictably and with such fine rigor, one would think that by now it had made an illuminated manuscript leaf of the "Kick me" sign taped to its back.

*

Inversions of the parabolistic: the toxic garden of Dr. Rappaccini, the toxicity of the Edenic, for that matter. Horticulturate the false positive and what have you unwittingly mundanitized?

*

Many mistake childhood for the "regency" period of an individual life, when they should look to middle age for signs of a vacated throne.

*

Somehow the world was painted over with statements, and now the world is lost. A thing covered over with statements, even a thing as immense as a world, simply will not be found. It is neither a matter of disproving the existence of large, ungainly totalities, nor of putting a halt to the unconsidered use of names for such totalities, but neither do considered worlds entertain grudges such that they might refuse to show themselves merely to spite the worldly ambitions of one person. And if you should try to search out an agent responsible for all of these assertions, this offending graffiti, what you will find in the end are only more assertions, these words for instance, which are every bit as much yours as someone else's. Why do you suppose they have remain hidden from you all this time, so far inside a *terra incognita* that they might as well have been furled up within a single hair on the head of someone worlds away? Yet the scroll tucked inside the hair is identical to the person lost in a world covered with his own statements . . . or someone else's. As I say, it makes no difference. One person's center is only another center's person. But that is to speak only of centers. And persons. What else is there? I'll tell you. But don't paint it. Stop painting.

*

I spend so much time getting what I want, there's no time left to do anything.

*

A metallurgist learns more by apprenticing to a weaver than the gold would like.

*

The insipidity of contemporary culture is profitably understood as a constant in a set of equations that describe public life in terms of profit and loss.

*

Perihelion in the orbit of the concept. Aphelion in the orbit of the object of the concept. Murk of gray matter between.

*

What we want is a better theory of equivalence, or better, an interfusion of theories, those of the grotesque and the equivalent. To hold a mirror up to the self, to take in unflinchingly the supreme hideousness—not of the self, but of the luxury to contemplate self, which gave rise to self.

*

The paean of Parmenides: just one more vulgar extraction from the impeccable (in-peckable) round. *The corpse eventually robs its own grave.*

*

Animal bipes implume, Plato called the grammatical species—a two-legged animal without feathers. The meaning of the designation captures less of our "truth" than its suggestively tripartite form: every two positive attributions require a negative one, as an ersatz regulative function in the absence of a regulating reality. Thus does language furnish us with wings—by telling us we have none. As for a more explicitly descriptive label, *animal quadrupes adrogans* should suffice, for with the disappearance of open spaces unmolested by ownership and "development," we withdraw farther and farther into the civilized pasturage of our words, which, by their oddly refractive properties, though they give us the appearance that we walk erect, have so successfully upended the theater of our endeavors as to reduce us to the cleverest but most presumptuous, and teeteringly perpendicularized, of ruminants. Presumptuous? Yes, because while we preen and luxuriate and make a Trimalchio's Feast out of even the most inconsequential desire, the vast number of cognitive stomachs through which the tiniest grain of providential humility must pass to reach our consciousness guarantees we will have swallowed the deadly thorn long before we know we have. Then again, at the time that the virgin continuum first suffered its anatomization into parts of speech, no one, neither vegetable nor animal nor god nor world, could conceive of so bizarre and destructive an innovation as self-consciousness, which then lay as far distant in the trackless, unspatialized future as our delivery from the ills and perils of self-consciousness seems to us now, lost as we are in the labyrinthine, suburban sprawl of that same future.

*

The invention of the circle: Such particularly fine notions as *life* will not be deterred from the creation of confections, for the sweet promise of a heaven they can no more deny themselves than water an unobstructed declivity to the level sea and, with serious hands, place their delicious glazed *summa* teetering on a spicule infinitely slender—and us all around in a ring to catch it when it falls.

*

The plague victim's mephitic breath, like all volcanic exhalations, is accompanied by a lava flow of unnaturally vivid tongue.

*

Touched, generate; retouched, regenerate; unretouched, unregenerate; reun-retouched, reunregenerate; unreunretouched, etc. The maintenance of norms *re*quires constant *re*qualification. *Re*member to pencil in the *re*bellion.

*

Political animal: what sight loves, sound rejects as touch. What touch can tolerate, smell will drop. It breaks into indistinguishable flavors. Shelter made of an emptiness: is *this* the comfort?

*

Prophecy in all its forms: an early—and obviously premature—optimism borne on the invention of the future tense and similar in ontology to the once oft-predicted, post-industrial three-day work week.

*

Moment of elk: stared at distant gas fire. Ate waldorf salad left over from airshow. Boys drifted by. Felt the old lift. Felt the lift leave. Heard barbecue-colored phone ringing inside barbecue-colored church. TV on curb. Doll on curb. *No shoes, no shirt, no service.* Shot elk from bedroom window. Moment of elk.

*

Drinking Song Under the Ordeal Tree: The mind's spills evade these cups. Noughts and havocs bite at their halters. Faces full of boiled god, selfdom in patches. Eyes two wingless phoebes suckling at rust. Sorrows tilled by ruin's allies. Bight of lambfrost 'round the rose. The resuscitated verb ploughed under. Red silk once for a love cry's sourdine. Now regret sealed in bitter cloves. Worn thread of belonging broken. Colors prove mercenary. Stale, the baptismal waters, which anneal only spite. Morning husbanded by salt storms. Day a wire bent around the black apple. The drilled gourd sieveth poisons. The wrong sword saveth the day. Sand babel of spoken worlds. Lessons under the ordeal tree.

*

Reverse Eden: perhaps the success curve of philosophy rises far more gradually than we might suppose, and only over the course of many, many generations will the results of its efforts actually bear a single piece of edible fruit. One must think not in terms of individual or even generational achievement, but rather the achievement of a species. Philosophy will only come into its own as our epitaph.

*

To exact the most vicious revenge it knows on an earlier mood, another mood merely follows.

*

Torture is the devil's poetry.

*

Ellipsis eclipsis ecthlipsis: I came around, was darkened, was liquidated. All of *I* is divided into three . . . more divisions, etc.

*

The statistical spread of variable opinion as to where the Playboy Bunny Siamese Twins in the upcoming Disney animation special should be joined serves as the most reliable index to the health of contemporary democratic institutions. This nation of ours: a torso with tongue for head licking and fondling its own breasts.

*

Eternity: or parasitical vine growing proximately along persons, though root and apical structures may extend from the basilary number fetish into a heavens complex respectively, and which often requires surgical adjustment through various cauteries of wonder and/or awe receptors.

*

Pictures form effortlessly in the mind because the mind is void of pictures.

*

To stare at an object until it's nothing but a congeries of colored patches, to repeat a word until all of its signifying force drains away, to reduce the great mass of organic response to axiomatic notions, to platonize, to drag race with death . . .

*

The martyrs to a hidden truth must plead for their own destruction.

*

The sacred moment waltzes lambward into self-slaughter. Being: a ritual scarification practiced among intoxicated premises.

*

Hives of activity are only the scrambled signal of uncertified indolence.

*

When disturbed, the oil beetle excretes a yellowish oily liquid from its leg joints. When a child goes missing, the grass-lined vacuoles in the human community fill with a shimmering, uncharacteristic concern.

*

Either we move and it doesn't, or it does, and "living" means the fuel it burns to keep us busy convincing ourselves that we're the ones doing the living.

*

In some hidden nook along the vast diapason of being, a petulant and neglected *Boredom that Follows Death* stands with his back to the glare of the divine empyrean, pissing on some metal dishes, from which vacant carillon, for age upon age, we have deduced the existence of angels.

*

Given the trend to reverse the traditional relation between individual and language— to claim that language takes us up, assumes us, rather than the reverse—one would be justified in the expectation that other conceptual traditions, especially within the political sphere, might in turn undergo a long awaited reversal. Yet that would be to adduce a factitious relation between us and our expectations. For no such relata exist, but we *are* just our expectations, and as such, though unwittingly, choose upon which sectors of experience to confer a tradition, in order to topple it sometime in the future. Rebellions are but platelets in the blood of the despot.

*

Package arrives for his death. His death opens package. Package contains his life.

*

Mother: the four-star generals that defecate shrapnel and cormorants, they too were once boys, and this dark mindless ice once water, these hands, this face in ribbons, the passivities turned to starvation—all that once fed on your sweet blood and breath.

*

If words were actually to rise to the expected level of fidelity with those circumstances to which they refer, we would never be able to find our way home.

*

Milk flows from rents in the cloth of privation.

*

Again, our average distance from the ground, from all stimulus, as determining the texture of our experience—We're far enough away from everything for desire to have enjoyed the luxuries of a remote empire unmolested by invasion, a perverse enclave of exotic architectures and milk-fed fauna, isolated in the mountains it has discharged around itself, not as an intentional means of defense, but just midden heaps of negations left over from the furious, coiled industry of its formation. Or better, it is from these steeps, these unnamed wastes and wilds, that we deduce the unobservable, exquisite center, our nougat, our *civitas dei*.

*

Weather represents the most distant yet still articulated interface between motivation and purposelessness; thus, it was the first god.

*

Time was once conceivable as the aspect and mood of the god verb: a durative tone, the texture of the feeling of movement through a resistant medium. Time has long since been conceivable as the god of *our* aspects and moods: a mercantile tone, the texture of the value of movement through a monetary medium.

*

These drugs should be stored in jars with child-proof caps. This effortless intelligence should be stored in an adult-proof life.

*

When moving in mechanical conveyance at certain velocities, one can choose whether, while staring out of a window, to capture each tree in the vision as it passes or to relax the eyes and invite the blur. By analogy, that stage in the development of consciousness at which the abstraction of time out of a sensual continuum becomes possible may be conceived of as a voluntary "strain" of thought arising from a specific "velocity" of experience. That is, it only occurs to consciousness at a certain "cultural speed" at which it moves through its world that it can choose to isolate *time* as a thematic object of thought—not too slow as to allow for constant and excessive scrutiny and consequent terror, nor so fast as to induce the blurred attitude of indifference. And yet this analogy no longer represents the situation accurately, for we have long since entered the epoch of tremendous stimulative velocity: it is no longer a question of how swiftly the parade of different individual objects pass before our vision; our sensorium is now as a blood-fed net of differential equations, coordinating evanscent webs of acceleration curves of sets of objects. And a consciousness must now ask itself, "How much effort am I willing to make to isolate and define . . . any single thing?" So was it only an historical curiosity, a perceptual mannerism, that we were so long entranced by the "unit," the primitive element? We are such dreams as stuff is made on.

*

Night calls a mountain a mare.

*

In perpetual transit, caged with vague anxieties, going only on the most fragile supposition that life's trajectory points in the direction of a resolution, even if an unintelligible, annihilating one. What we consider our habitude of uncertainty and rootlessness would intoxicate the wolf with its stability.

*

By shivering we can hold in the precious heat without need of hands or instruction— the amanual, untaught arts that educate us into a living, a graspable form.

*

The unlived examination is worth examining.

*

Relax: sooner or later each of us gets to play the D.A., don't you worry, and watch from a teal sofa while the trousers of the terrified perp harden into a bud vase of piranhas and make soft gravel out of his legs. *I* watches, *you* trembles—by definition—that is, until it's my turn, and it always is.

*

Until a thumb approach, the thimble bee will moot at a glabrous leaf.

*

The phonemes, the words and sentences, all utterances uttered at all times simultaneously, such sound as comprises a catacoustic net by which we find our way in our dark: fruit bats in the crate of consciousness ferried across oceans of—

*

Hapax legomenon: say something once and nothing will have been said. Anything that has been said has already been said an infinite number of times. The utterance is born fully grown on a foam of world-engendering constraints.

*

To the east of a window in my room, a cloud very gradually passes in front of the sun, at first eliminating, then deepening the contrast between light and shade on the side of a house across the street. Soon the light areas grow brighter, and, by a sympathy of perception, the shadows cast by a neighboring forsythia appear to grow darker, and with these gathering antitheses, the speed at which they intensify would seem also to increase. All the while I sit here and secretly wish that such a clash of values might continue without abatement, until the luminous areas were white hot with a brilliance dangerous to look upon, and the dark patches gaped toward depths irreconcilable with the dimensions of a suburban milieu. The wish, too, begins simultaneously to warm and deepen the retinal amphitheaters themselves, so that I have every reason to expect that in the next several seconds those surfaces upon which these images are projected will ignite and my entire visual field engulf itself in every sort of conflagration imaginable . . . I'll hazard you weren't aware that there were varieties of conflagration, but yes, you will find them among the prodigies nurtured by an angry man sitting in a dark cellar held hostage by his words.

*

The first ordeal: names, these rude bits of cool fearlessness against the counterblast, so that ever after we might pass through all that is given us, presuming to have taken it; so that the first ordeal of taking, torn into names, shall mend itself, if torn again, again the accursed mending, with a tale for a scar.

*

The depicted blur—as in the paintings of G. Richter, or in films the deliberate adjustment of focus to indicate that a character has been drugged, a blur minus the feeling in the eyes—stands in like relation to the authentic blur as warnings from the old about the fleetingness of time to the actual fleetingness of time.

*

The time required for me to explain the time required for me to time required for me time required for time required . . . *time*.

*

Future in front for the sake of dispensations behind and nothing ever where we are. Where is "We are?"

*

After luxuriating over the retouched thigh of the porn model, the camera recedes, and what was thought to be thigh is revealed, as if in a dream, to have been the brushed steel surface of an upscale appliance.

*

The drupe of desire: only in the capital will a cosmopolite find that fruit properly prepared—a mesocarp of pinguid, interpenetrating and translucent joys struggling to close a scissors into their midsections—whose inedibility provides a boundless feast.

*

Water feels as hard as concrete when hit at great speed. We hold the ground up by our feet.

*

Imperfection of heights sluiced into humble embrace of adjacent valleys. The habit of stupidity is as ravenous as the satiety of wisdom.

*

Protagoras redux: symmetrical along a vertical axis, suspended from a load-bearing spine, with a bulb at the top, as of an inverted thermometer—the measure of all things because all of its mercury has drained out of it.

*

I can hear me hearing me all the way down.

*

The Silent Majority revisited: consider all the loud powers, all the bombast and sporting propensities, that a moss disrelishes instinctively. It has nothing to prove; its ambitions remain plumb to the hushed campaign of its propagation. The mild love it inspires, its dream to achieve a cute, yearbook inscription-like ubiquity, cannot help but make for a supple sense of self, and, voila! it's everywhere, carpeting the sills and lobes of the wetter world like a soft pavement, but cool to the feet, offering enticements that would soon scorch its delicate benignity with shame, were the vigilance—bristling, supine—with which it deals out its moisture not the perfect expression of ruthlessness.

*

Lux + ferre = *Lucifer, or Light bearer, meaning Venus, when appearing as the morning star*: a bioluminescence or "cold light" produced along the underside of the 6th and the 7th abdominal segments of Lampyridae (e.g. the glow worm) is the result of a chemical reaction, the oxidation of *luciferin* by its companion enzyme, *luciferase*. Why is it that a bug will make light of a devil, while we make a devil out of light?

*

Nature carves and enamels its canines to resemble "ladybugs" so exactly that we come to have "ladybugs" by forgetting, or never knowing, nature's unquenchable blood thirst—the thirstier, the more unassuming. "Look mommy, a ladybug!"

*

However cool the nocturnal mischief of political manipulation, still it does throw a complement of sparks, which most of us see yet persist in taking for meteors. And that we continue to refer to meteors as "falling stars" suggests that our common dream of self-determination is farther off than we would like to, are able to, think.

*

The Brutus that expelled the tyrant and forged a republic carried his day by making careful allowances for the eventual appearance of a Livy.

*

The open, inviting lips of the categories to which we have entrusted our thoughts are in actuality the most ruthless of whetstones. While they blow their kisses and seduce with *come hither*-like whispers about the structure of the real, rows of hidden teeth are furtively sharpened.

*

The crowning of the natal real: we share the birth pangs of an incomprehensible matrix when we ache in the presence of beauty. What cannot be understood can be converted—into pain.

*

When I grow up I want to be president: the extraordinary resourcefulness of nature only serves to encourage the thug from the hills—properly our vestigial male infancy—to assume that anything that doesn't hit back can be carried off, expropriated, raped—just one more Sabine woman in a finger painting from our formative, "classical" age.

*

Strange indeed that the world should knock before opening your door, but arrives so suddenly, always without notice, and you would rather leave—but of course you cannot—and you think to yourself, "Oh, for a crank-operated table setting—glasses, *flatware, lacquered meal, etc., glued to under-surface, then simply crank works into position, in which process flints are struck and light slightly-burned-down candles. I'll simply apologize, politely return the world to its deluge, say that I'm not alone, that I have company coming.*" And the world will wink, "*Maybe another time.*"

*

How admirably the ebb and flow of crowds would serve as an abacus to the day, if only the day possessed hands.

*

It is left for us to inveigle a destiny from our own mismeasurements.

*

To equate fully sunlight and starlight is to conceive of the daytime as that strange, unnatural glow that often precedes a cataclysm.

*

The failure of music: my trumpet I have smashed on the millstone, my cymbal pounded into a strongbox. I sleep on my drum, and will, with the sunrise, hang myself from the gibbet-harp. Bury me in the piano I took for a steppe that opened onto no further word.

*

Nursery of "No!": for the longest time only minor detours of scent, vague *almosts*—at most, an occasional *not quite*, agitated the empty plenitude of the beast awareness. Then came the two-legged logician and his tilde, and the violent accession of unfettered comparison.

*

I day-by-day it, without a choice in the matter, but apparently I day-ed it once too often, became a self. Woe is self.

*

The biblical God's hydrogen burns from the pressurized center of our godlessness, but the true god swims in hydrogen's unthinking centerlessness.

*

To train oneself to listen for the cadences of consciousness shut off from our awareness because they innerve our awareness, to quiet oneself before the whirr and click of escapements and finely milled pinions and splines inside the *I am*, to train one's ears on the low grinding of metal against metal within the *virtually* self-transparent, to learn to distinguish the fabrication from the fabrication's fabrications, among the latter of which would include the putative silence outside the work of fabricating (or so the fabricator suspects).

*

Decent, fear-loving people must kill to protect the honor of their fears.

*

The stupidity to continue looking; to hold out for what no language ever could say; that idiotic intransigence; the moronic hope that something might turn up other than what the authorities, the expectations, could expect; that insufferable mulishness thanks to which we have such ellipses in the grand march of clever facility as Max Beckmann and Anton Bruckner . . . and, of course, the mules themselves.

*

Ecce homo: remove a little bit of cortical hardware, and suddenly they're no longer in command of their pronouns.

*

The unintended you prefers that a bit more of who you think you are elapse before it engulfs and not-you-s the next portion of you in line to be disowned in your ongoing, federally funded effort to remain whole.

*

Omphalos: whenever the urge comes over me to improve my state, I find I have always already sworn myself to the inexorabilities of the present, thus to have determined it *my world*, having named my plenitude of awareness 'til all lay outside of me, in piles of names—over there—and I, over here, a perfectly vacant equilibrium. Like the man who steals a car from the factory, part by part, I have rebuilt myself outside of the world, without disturbing it in the least—perhaps a slight pucker at the site of my removal. One will have accomplished this without so much as knowing. The world, once mine—or properly, my nameless substance, now reconstituted entirely of names—lies before me, without me—my only possession.

*

Me I could do without. You, however—you remain indispensable . . . then again, only to me. I speak of a you less specific than an actual companion, less generalized than a concept of personhood. Everyone "has" a you and a me—not by choice, not a you according to the me's dictates, yet a me forged in the glow of you. Nor will we find that centrifuge in the form of a stronger verb than "has" that could separate out into possessor and possessed these thoroughly confused elements; a more vivid word would only constrain the easy transmissibility that allows us to represent ourselves in such impersonal and—more to the point—convenient terms. The government of personal pronouns goes to great lengths to maintain a bland, unremarkable surface of signification, an Eisenhower-like rectitude and sleepy competence, but beware the debilitary-pronominal complex that lurks beneath these expediencies, providing and denying certitudes according as one's faith in stable identities wanes and waxes. Thus the tides of our lunacy, governed by little words.

*

Now means its own brave demolition more than I have ever meant me.

*

Not the changeling who moves, but the changeling's house.

*

Stray flares from the festival of lights that stream and flicker behind closed eyes have been detected at the rim of the conceivable universe.

*

No happier systematic doubt persists than the one everybody refuses to entertain.

*

Enlightenments break through the rigid shell of our animal tenacities with a rhythm every bit as precise as the delivery of sensitive, heavily redacted government documents to the public scrutiny.

*

One may notice that in cases where one is pleased, one finds oneself pleased to have noticed that, in order to find oneself pleased, one will have left off with trying to think of one's self as pleased or with thinking of one's self for that matter, or with thinking for that matter.

*

The right to be considered meaningful feeds the ambitions of every sound, yet only the rare hydrated purr between vibratile surfaces is awarded residency within the gated community of speech.

*

Keep your passion for the infinite vestaled, *sopraporta*, behind the red letters of the "Exit" sign your next breath makes of the achieved flesh.

*

No matter the direction or length of my pilgrimage, I am always walking in the hand of a method that in holding its palm open refuses to know me, thinking I might know enough to guide it out of the hand in which it too is trapped. Hands inside of refusals, providing, guarding—doing things that bear no resemblance to a refusal. Pilgrimages inside of hands—bearing us toward neither shrine nor provision, yet doing so with a full, devout heart.

*

A doctrine concerning the Buoyant Heart has been set adrift in a cask of blood—a bit of itself to eat each day, a quantity of blood to wash itself down, and a rhythm to mark the autophagy, dotted with the trembling sources of unacknowledged hungers. Admonitions that nothing be spared to keep afloat this doctrine of the heart's necessary buoyancy circulate like a sentinel lymph among the letters of the doctrine. And hollowing out the vowels of these warnings: a cargo of chained hands, clawing their way toward a relative utopia, where hope is measured in units of chain, where the unhoped-for word cannot be forgotten, nor the unspoken hope forgiven.

*

The master of any rite is forbidden to witness it. By rite we mean any form of verification. We mean all perception. By a blindness of rites, we mean.

*

Geological survey: since it has not suffered the fatal *ecstasis* of voluntary movement, as horizonless as it is still, the mineral memory exults through dense systems of modular recollection latticed along arrogant, motiveless integrities, and urged by gracious easements in the closed earth, gives up an occasional (soon to be prostituted) gleam to this peculiar layer of awareness the "laughing animal" chose to inhabit soon after the dove returned to the ark with its legs shackled through a hole in its beak.

*

Dolphins and tuna: the vagaries of living threaten our way of life. A passing mood has established its own state flower and bird, each hour is busy carving a motto into its forearm, every individual breath must stand on line to register its serial number as an indemnity against the waves of deniers that beat individual things into a submission of indistinctness, against which the deniers themselves are helpless, caught as they are in their own mood, the same seine of hours and breaths.

*

I have taken up the task of being the last thing hereabout and feel the great distance between us holding out in front of me the awareness that very soon I am to be alone. It was not among my intentions, whenever I last had them out, to be the only one left, but I cannot be sure of this. I am so busy guarding my intentions whenever I air them, that I never have a chance either to count or examine them with the least scrutiny. For all I know, many of my intentions might not even belong to me. They could as well have been the possession of another who had them out and I saw a few that I liked and understood them as belonging to me. In fact, some of them may even have sub-intentions all their own. Perhaps several intentions are busy inside me, building my awareness of them, exactly the way I keep busy out here, guarding them, wondering if they're mine, wishing I knew them better. Perhaps it is my intentions who wish for me to be the last thing. That way I will have no reason to go on guarding them. I will finally have the freedom, the luxury, to scrutinize my intentions, perhaps even mother them a little. But by then, they will already have run away.

*

And in precious torrents of a creole only half-understood, each passing instant dies equivocating as to who is passing whom, while we lie awake at night unable to sleep, wishing the roots of it all were really the roots of it all.

*

Each passing day crystallizes into a memory, and every grain of memory fills in an originary Nile, whose inundation once watered our serene, faultless beginning. One's navel is his Valley of Kings.

*

Into the lake of the mouth, one syllable at a time, I followed a retrograde umbilicus hand over hand back to my thoracic Eurydice.